Corker

Wendy Lill

Talonbooks
1998

Talonbooks
#104—3100 Production Way
Burnaby, British Columbia, Canada V5A 4R4

Typeset in New Baskerville and printed and bound in Canada by Hignell
Printing.

First Printing: September 1998

Talonbooks are distributed in Canada by General Distribution Services,
325 Humber College Blvd., Toronto, Ontario, Canada M9W 7C3;
Tel.:(416) 213-1919; Fax:(416) 213-1917.

Talonbooks are distributed in the U.S.A. by General Distribution
Services Inc., 85 Rock River Drive, Suite 202, Buffalo, New York, U.S.A.
14207-2170; Tel.:1-800-805-1083; Fax:1-800-481-6207.

Canadian Cataloguing in Publication Data

Lill, Wendy, 1950-
    Corker

    A play.
    ISBN 0-88922-394-7

    I. Title.
PS8573.I429C67 1998   C812'.54   C98-910718-3
PR9199.3.L517C67 1998

To Sam Starr—my fellow traveller

ACKNOWLEDGEMENTS

Corker came about with the assistance of many good people. I want to thank Claudy Levy, Karen Llewellyn, Norman Llewellyn and Marilyn Aucoin for their contribution to this story. As always, I want to thank Mary Vingoe, my friend and Artistic Director, the production crew as well as the original cast—Gay Hauser, John Dunsworth, Joan Orenstein, Michael Peterson, Ryan Rogerson and Peter Blais. Many of the most colourful lines in the play grew out of their dedicated work which continued right up until opening night and made that night and the memory of that night—forever joyful.

Corker was first produced by the Eastern Front Theatre Company, February 19 to March 1, 1998 at Neptune Theatre's DuMaurier Stage, Halifax, Nova Scotia with the following cast and crew:

MERIT	Gay Hauser
LEONARD	John Dunsworth
FLORENCE	Joan Orenstein
GAL	Michael Peterson
CORKER	Ryan Rogerson
GLENNY	Peter Blais

Director	Mary Vingoe
Technical Director	Michael Hogan
Assistant Technical	Gary Joseph
Music	Paul Cram
Production Dramaturge	Leslie Hennen
Stage Manager	Jane Butler
Assistant Stage Manager	Tammy Williams
Set and Costume Design	Gary Markle
Lighting Designer	Leigh Ann Vardy
Crew	John Shurko

CHARACTERS

Merit MacPhee, 45
Leonard Mills, 47, Merit's husband
Florence MacPhee, 75, Merit's mother
Gal (Galahad) MacPhee, 40, Merit's brother
Glenny, a social worker
Corker, an outsider

SETTING

Halifax, mid-nineties

* Notes on the set: the greenery in the Solarium has to be substantial enough to double as a park in Act Two. The piano should be on wheels for easy movement about the room.

ACT ONE

SCENE ONE

*Lights up on a funeral in an inner-city Catholic church. There
are just shadows of icons, vestiges of ceremony. The 'Song of
Farewell' is just finishing. LEONARD, MERIT, FLORENCE and
GAL stand looking slightly upward. LEONARD, in a three-piece
suit, holds MERIT's arm lightly, his face inscrutable. MERIT,
dressed in a smart black coat and hat. Crisp, unsentimental.
Great high heels but they are bothering her. She shifts about trying
to get relief. Her brother GAL, in his best sports jacket, holds
FLORENCE's arm protectively. FLORENCE, the grieving mother,
sniffs quietly. GAL takes out a pack of Tictacs, takes some, holds
them out to his mother, who shakes her head slightly, then holds
them out to MERIT, who glares at him so fiercely he quickly
pockets them.*

VOICE OF PRIEST:
To you, O Lord, we commend the soul of Serena MacPhee,
your servant; in the sight of this world she is now dead; in
your sight may she live forever. Forgive whatever sins she
committed through human weakness and in your goodness
grant her everlasting peace. In the name of the Father, the
Son and the Holy Spirit.

*MERIT, FLORENCE and GAL kneel, cross themselves. LEONARD
remains standing.*

VOICE OF PRIEST:
And now, before we close, if you will permit a slight break in
tradition, Serena left me a note with some final thoughts to
share with you.

FLORENCE looks up hopefully. MERIT is astounded.

FLORENCE:
Thank God!

LEONARD:
(whispers to MERIT) Did you know about this?

MERIT:
No! Of course not!

VOICE OF PRIEST:
The last words of Serena MacPhee: "Life is a struggle but in the middle of it, there's joy. Find the joy. Chase it down. Flat out, even if you're scared shitless."

MERIT:
(clenching her teeth) Good God.

VOICE OF PRIEST:
"And money? Screw money! Money's not important. Community's important. Family's important. What did I learn? Not nearly enough but here goes. Roll your corncob in butter. Lick your plate clean."

FLORENCE:
I remember that.

MERIT:
I'm going to be sick.

VOICE OF PRIEST:
"Never shut a door in someone's face. Don't crowd people at the grocery store. Don't ram your cart up against another. Don't even use a grocery cart. Shop every day for what you need. Live every day. Make your own beer, but don't drink it all like I did."

MERIT starts to leave, LEONARD holds her arm tightly.

VOICE OF PRIEST:
"Never let a stray cat go hungry. Call your mother once a week. *(FLORENCE begins to sob. GAL hands her a large tissue.)* Learn something new every day. Ask more questions. Why are so many people allergic to peanuts suddenly? Have peanuts changed? Have people changed? Seek wisdom and tell the truth. Stand on your head once in a while. And laugh. Every day. Laugh! And dance…if you got an ounce of energy left…. Dance…."

The sound of a scratchy record begins. MERIT's eyes widen. The triumphant sound of David Bowie's voice booms out 'Let's Dance.' LEONARD and MERIT are startled, incredulous.

MERIT:
  (under her breath) Unbelievable.

GAL:
  Holy shit.

  FLORENCE smiles, starts to sway with the music.

MERIT:
  Mom!

PRIEST:
  And now we'll form a long chain and weave around the sanctuary then downstairs to the hall for coffee and sandwiches. Turn to your left. Hands on the hips in front of you. All together now. Once more for Serena.

MERIT:
  I won't. I will not.

LEONARD:
  Just do it, Merit. Please.

  MERIT reluctantly turns. LEONARD puts his hands on her hips. FLORENCE puts hers on MERIT's and so on. GAL gets into it, as if harking back to the good old drunken snake dance days of his university fraternity. MERIT and LEONARD do as little as possible. The four look like some kind of reluctant hapless chorus line.

SCENE TWO

An upscale south end Halifax home. The livingroom opens onto a solarium where a fountain splutters into a jungle of indoor greenery. A wrought iron bench beckons. A glass door leads out into a garden. The livingroom is perfectly appointed and never used. A beat-up upright piano, painted with peace symbols, sits incongruously in the centre of the room. There is a desk stacked with papers, off to one side, several pairs of women's shoes piled beside it. The livingroom opens into a hall. MERIT enters, agitated, hurriedly takes off her hat and coat. She takes off her shoes and throws them in a corner, grabs some comfortable ones.

She stops at the piano, glares at it, starts moving it around, making it less conspicuous.

MERIT:

Love life. Live every day. Find the joy. Chase it down! Thank you sister for your old hippie clichés. And thanks for your final pronouncement about stray cats. That's what the world needs now—better fed cats. And stand on your head. Who the hell has time to stand on their head?

LEONARD enters, going through the mail.

LEONARD:

Visa bill

MERIT:

Screw Visa.

LEONARD:

Mastercard.

MERIT:

Screw Mastercard.

LEONARD:

Gal's going to put the touch on us again. I could see that look in his eyes—And your mom's way out there in true MacPhee fashion. I heard her tell the organist it was a heart attack, the Priest cancer and some guy in sweatpants that it was food poisoning. We really should try to....

MERIT:

I can't deal with that now. *(checks her watch)* It's almost five o'clock. I'd better call in. Plug in the kettle and throw some Peek Freans on a plate. And could you get me some Aspirins and Rolaids?

LEONARD exits. MERIT pushes the piano further towards the wall, then picks up the phone.

MERIT:

P.V.? I'm back from the funeral. The family is on the way, One more hour of wet Kleenexes and red noses and remember whens and then I'm back on track. What's up?

The doorbell rings and MERIT opens it to FLORENCE and GAL.
GAL is dancing around, humming to himself.

GAL:
"Put on your red dress baby...." Here mom, let me take your coat.

MERIT:
(to phone) Tell him I can't see him until after the budget. Tell him nobody cares abut heritage buildings now. No don't tell him that. Just put him off. *(to FLORENCE)* Leonard's getting tea. I'll just be a sec.

GAL walks into the livingroom, sees the solarium.

GAL:
(to FLORENCE) Will ya look at that. They've put in a jungle.

MERIT:
Solarium. Had it put in this fall. Where are Margaret and the boys?

GAL:
She had business at the bank, dropped the boys at a hockey game. *(quietly)* Merit, I've got to talk to you. We've got a bit of a....

MERIT:
Not now Gal.

GAL:
Well it's...

MERIT:
(fierce) Not now!

GAL, cowed, turns his attention to his mother.

GAL:
Are you warm enough mom? Could I get your sweater from the car.

FLORENCE:
I'm fine.

She walks over to the piano, rubs the top of it.

FLORENCE:

> *(to MERIT)* I'm glad you took the piano. Serena loved that piano.

MERIT:

> I had no choice. The Sally Ann didn't want it.

FLORENCE:

> You could fix it up a bit. You could put it right over there by the....

MERIT:

> No I can't. *(cuts her off)* I'll find a place for it. There are women's shelters, places like that. Don't worry mom, I'll handle it. *(to phone)* Tell the Nellie McClung Society the gender issue is dead, to quit whining and try harder.

FLORENCE:

> She kept checking her watch at the funeral. Her phone rang while she was viewing the body. It was eerie. Where should I sit?

GAL:

> This one's not too bad, mom. I sat in it at Easter.

MERIT:

> *(to phone)* Tell them we're on a tight schedule. I need each department's numbers by next Friday. I want someone there to defend every line item. Defend it or lose it.

FLORENCE:

> She sounds like she's fighting a war.

GAL:

> She is sort of. The new Premier's a wingnut. They're cutting programs right and left. Everyone's trying to position themselves so they don't go down. But she's doing alright. My little sis. They call her The Slasher. *(looks around)* 'Cept I sure as hell wouldn't want a fountain in my livingroom.

FLORENCE:

> I would. It's like being in the Garden of Eden.

MERIT:

   (to phone) What is it? What? Take the line. It's alright. I'll wait. No, I'll wait.

   LEONARD returns with a tray with tea, an ice bucket etc.

MERIT:

   (to LEONARD) P.V. thinks something's up in the Premier's office. *(to phone)* I'm on hold. What? He what? He cancelled the Chinese delegation. That was booked months.... They are what? Sitting at Customs.

LEONARD:

   Easy Merit. Tea Florence?

FLORENCE:

   Thank you.

MERIT:

   (to phone) What do you mean? No one went to meet them?

FLORENCE:

   Who's she talking to?

LEONARD:

   Her executive assistant.

FLORENCE:

   I thought that's what you were.

LEONARD:

   (to GAL) Scotch?

GAL:

   You bet.

   LEONARD puts some ice in a glass, pours GAL and himself a drink.

LEONARD:

   (quietly) Get off the phone.

MERIT:

   (to LEONARD) I've got to find out what.... *(to phone)* He's what? *(to LEONARD)* He's golfing with the Chair of the Power Corp. and a consultant from that American think tank....

GAL:

I guess you hear it here first eh? Action central.

LEONARD:

Get off the phone.

GAL:

(holds out his empty glass) Any more where that came from?

LEONARD takes the glass, goes to liquor cabinet and pours another.

GAL:

I see your law firm got shut out of the amalgamation work. That musta hurt. Guess you were backing the wrong horse, eh? Believe me I've been there. I live there. I've got a permanent address there. *(tries again)* Think there's gonna be a cabinet shuffle? Being in small business, you're always wondering if you're kissing the right ass at Economic Renewal. So whatdiya think?

LEONARD:

No idea. Get off the phone.

MERIT:

There are three media crews following them around the course. Something is definitely happening.

LEONARD:

Get off the....

MERIT:

There are fifteen Chinese businessmen sitting in Customs...I....

LEONARD:

(takes the phone, speaks into it) P.V., call us back when you know something. *(puts down the phone, to MERIT)* There's been a death in the family.

MERIT, still distracted by her telephone conversation, turns her attention to her guests.

MERIT:
Right. So! Everyone looked after? Have some Peek Freans. We'd better eat them up. They'll just go stale around here.

FLORENCE:
Sit down, Merit.

MERIT perches on the edge of a chair.

FLORENCE:
Sit please.

MERIT sits right down in a chair.

FLORENCE:
You haven't been Up Home in a long time.

MERIT:
I'm sorry but it's just crazy now at work.

FLORENCE:
Serena was up the weekend before her stroke. I got caught up on all her news. If we didn't talk once a week, I just felt lost.

MERIT:
Did I have those Aspirins yet?

LEONARD:
Yes.

FLORENCE:
You haven't seen the donut shop yet. The drive-thru is right below your bedroom window.

MERIT glares at GAL. He looks sheepish.

MERIT:
Really. I sort of liked the orchard. *(GAL winces)*

FLORENCE:
Oh well, times change. No point in crying over spilt milk. You work too hard.

MERIT:

In two weeks, we're going on a holiday. I'm counting the days. Two weeks 'til Costa Rica. Rum punches and warm sand. Far from the madding crowd. We've got a beautiful little gem of a place right on the beach.

Phone rings. MERIT jumps it.

MERIT:

Hello. *(listens)* The carpets aren't dirty! *(slams down the phone)* You look tired mom. Would you like to lie down?

GAL:

That's a good idea. Have a lie down. Get a bit of kip before we head back.

FLORENCE:

I'm fine thank you.

MERIT:

There's a daybed in the study.

FLORENCE:

I don't want to lie down. I want to talk.

MERIT:

I thought you'd be all talked out after all those hours of….

FLORENCE:

(interrupts) I mean as a family…what she meant to us. Something we remember that we'll carry with us forever.

MERIT is impatient, exasperated.

MERIT:

Well I really think that….

LEONARD:

(warning) Merit….

MERIT:

Well I guess we could do that.

GAL:

Who wants to start?

FLORENCE:
I remember when she won the Miss Antigonish pageant.
Standing there with her shiny hair and that armful of
roses—then she burst into tears and ran home. She couldn't
bear to see the heartbreak on the faces of the other girls who
didn't win. And she gave back her crown.

GAL:
And started wearing those bag dresses that covered every
inch of her. Drove my friends crazy. They all had crushes on
her.

FLORENCE:
Remember how she shopped at Frenchie's.

MERIT:
I shopped at Frenchie's.

FLORENCE:
But not like Serena. She made an art of shopping at
Frenchie's. You were always looking at the clothes on the
next rack, not at the one in front of you. You were always
looking for something better.

MERIT:
What's wrong with that?

LEONARD:
Nothing.

FLORENCE:
I never asked. Was there a will?

LEONARD:
There wasn't anything to leave.

MERIT:
Fifty years old and nothing to put in a will. How depressing.

LEONARD:
Well there were the notes. Gal and I found notes.

FLORENCE:
Notes?

GAL:

There was a note to the woman next door to take her plants.

GAL takes some buttons from his jacket.

GAL:

And one to my boys to have her shoebox full of buttons. Here's a couple of them *(reads buttons)* 'Ban the Bomb,' 'Refuse the Cruise,' 'I think therefore I must be NDP.' This one says 'Beauty Kills Bunnies.'

FLORENCE:

How thoughtful.

MERIT:

(pointedly, to FLORENCE) Well, given the fact that she wrote notes and gave the Priest her final thoughts, I guess maybe one would have to deduce that....

FLORENCE:

She wasn't leaving anything to chance. Since it can happen any minute—a bus can hit you, or a meteor, or a big ice ball. I read about a farmer in Kansas out walking in his field and he was struck dead by an ice ball. That's why it's good to have your affairs in order.

MERIT and LEONARD look at each other. GAL looks at his empty glass.

GAL:

Let's have another drink.

LEONARD pours him a drink.

GAL:

I remember how she loved to play tricks on people.

MERIT:

She went out of her way to get my goat.

FLORENCE:

Because it was so gettable.

GAL:

Remember the time she put marijuana in dad's pipe.

FLORENCE:

He liked it alright.

MERIT:

She was the first person Up Home to ever get charged with possession. She had a criminal record at eighteen.

FLORENCE:

Merit, we are here to honour her memory.

MERIT:

I'm sorry. I'm just tired. It's been a long week. I didn't appreciate bunny hopping around the church with a bunch of street people.

FLORENCE:

It was her way of saying goodbye. She wanted us to be all together. Laughing, dancing.

MERIT:

I don't have time to be laughing and dancing with a bunch of bums....

FLORENCE:

You could have at least talked to them. You might have got some comfort from it.

MERIT:

I doubt that.

FLORENCE:

She wanted it to be a celebration.

MERIT:

It was a fiasco.

LEONARD:

(warning) Merit....

FLORENCE:

We're here to honour her memory.

MERIT:

I have been honouring it all week. I've just....

LEONARD:
> *(warning)* Merit.

> *The phone rings. MERIT jumps for it.*

MERIT:
> *(Listens to phone, to LEONARD)* He's just announced he's privatizing the power company. That's gonna change all the numbers...everything. I'd better do some damage control.

LEONARD:
> Excuse me, Florence. I should make a couple of calls myself.

> *LEONARD walks over to the side of the room, picks up another phone.*

GAL:
> Oh what the hell.

> *GAL reaches into his coat jacket, takes out a pager, starts taking his messages.*

LEONARD:
> *(to phone)* I want to get a hold of any contracts pending....

MERIT:
> *(to phone)* I want you to get on the phone and make sure the department figures don't start changing in the process.

> *Abandoned, FLORENCE drinks her tea. There is a faint knock at the door but no one notices. The door opens. CORKER walks in. He is a small man, just over five feet tall. Indeterminate age. He could have Down's Syndrome but, if not, some other physical or facial mannerisms which set him apart. He scratches his hand nervously. CORKER sees MERIT's jacket hanging on the back of a chair. He walks by and drops it on the floor. He stares at MERIT who is marching back and forth, telephone in hand. CORKER sees the piano. He rushes over to it and puts his cheek against it. FLORENCE notices him first.*

FLORENCE:
> I saw you at the funeral.

CORKER:
> Gonta heaven.

MERIT notices him, lets out a gasp.

MERIT:
Who are you?

CORKER:
(frightened) GONTA HEAVEN!

LEONARD:
How did you get in here?

MERIT:
Oh my God!

CORKER, frightened by the attention, jumps up on the chesterfield.

CORKER:
GONTA HEAVEN! GONTA HEAVEN.

FLORENCE:
Don't scare him.

LEONARD:
Careful. He might have a weapon.

CORKER:
Gonta heaven.

GAL:
I don't think he's all there.

FLORENCE:
Don't be afraid. We won't hurt you.

LEONARD:
Everyone stay calm.

CORKER looks back and forth from FLORENCE to MERIT.

CORKER:
(mutters slowly as if memorized) Gi a to ah. Gi a to ah.

MERIT:
What are you saying?

CORKER pulls out a piece of paper from his coat, shoves it towards MERIT.

CORKER:
Gi a to ah.

MERIT:
What is it?

CORKER:
(pushing it in her direction) Gi a to ah.

MERIT:
Give it to her.

She walks up and takes it from him.

LEONARD:
What is it?

MERIT:
A note.

MERIT opens it, reads it.

LEONARD:
What does it say?

MERIT looks up. CORKER retreats fearfully to a corner, crouches down shivering.

MERIT:
It says: "Take care of Corker. Love, Serena."

CORKER retreats fearfully to a corner, crouches down shivering, looking straight at MERIT.

CORKER:
(mutters) Reena.

SCENE THREE

Two hours later. FLORENCE is sitting on one side of the fountain, CORKER on the other. Around CORKER are empty cracker boxes, pop cans, fruit peelings. He is staring at MERIT as she paces about the livingroom, note clutched in her hand.

FLORENCE:
(placing a plastic container into the water) Let's pretend it's the ferry going across the harbour. I'll be Halifax. You be Dartmouth. I'll push it to you. You push it back.

MERIT is pacing back and forth in the livingroom, the note still clutched in her hand. GAL has been pouring himself some drinks. He screws up his courage, approaches MERIT.

GAL:
I guess since we got some time….

MERIT:
Not here.

GAL:
I mean why don't we just go into the….

MERIT:
(seething) Not now!

GAL pours himself another drink. CORKER picks up the floating container and hurls it across the floor, water flying. GAL retrieves it.

MERIT:
(glowering at CORKER) Were you born in a barn?

FLORENCE:
(to CORKER) How 'bout you be Halifax?

She floats the boat again. CORKER seems happy with this arrangement. He floats it back to her, all the time staring at MERIT. She looks over at LEONARD who is reading the 'Globe and Mail.'

MERIT:
Look at the mess he's making. He just keeps staring at me. And look at mom over there 'bonding' with him. I should be on the phone. I should be in bed getting a good sleep so that I can face the onslaught tomorrow.

The doorbell rings. MERIT is relieved. LEONARD puts the paper away, stands. He goes to the door, opens it to GLENNY, who is in a 50s bomber jacket, rumpled sweatshirt. GLENNY extends his hand.

GLENNY:

Albert Glenny. Sorry it took so long. I was....

LEONARD avoids the hand.

LEONARD:

(curt, cuts him off) My wife and I would be grateful if you would just get him out of here.

MERIT:

(jumps in) I called social services two hours ago.... I said it was an emergency. What if he'd taken an axe to all of us?

They look at CORKER who is floating containers in the fountain.

GLENNY:

Doesn't look like he did.

MERIT:

Well he could have.

GLENNY:

I was at another emergency. At the middle of a bridge. Is this more of an emergency?

MERIT hesitates. GLENNY approaches CORKER.

GLENNY:

Let's head out, Cork. We don't want to bother these good people any longer.

CORKER picks up the container full of water and throws it across the floor.

GLENNY:

If I had a looney for every time he throws things, I'd be a looniare.

FLORENCE:

Not to worry. Just water. Is his real name Corker?

GLENNY:

Ah...no. It's Billy Cork. Corker for short.

CORKER:

Suck me!

GAL:
Did you hear that?

LEONARD:
Get him out of here.

CORKER:
(right to LEONARD) Suck me!

GLENNY:
He knows how to get a rise out of people.

CORKER:
Suck suck suck suck!

MERIT:
My mother can't deal with things like this right now. We've just….

FLORENCE:
It's alright. I've heard it before.

CORKER:
Gonta heaven. GONTA HEAVEN!

FLORENCE:
I bet she told him that's where she was going.

GLENNY:
Pardon?

FLORENCE:
My daughter. He was at her funeral. I saw him there.

GLENNY:
Serena MacPhee was your daughter?

FLORENCE:
Did you know her?

GLENNY:
Yes. I was going to the funeral….

FLORENCE:
Then there was an emergency at the middle of the bridge.

GLENNY:
   That's right.

FLORENCE:
   How did he know Serena?

GLENNY:
   She just saw him one day wandering around and took him
   home.

MERIT:
   That sounds about right. I'm Serena's sister. It's been a long
   day and we'd be very grateful if you'd just....

FLORENCE:
   Does he have a family? Where's his mother?

GLENNY:
   She died a year ago.

FLORENCE:
   What about his father?

GLENNY:
   He was too ill to take care of him so he gave him up.

FLORENCE:
   That poor man.

MERIT:
   Mom, I think we should just stay out of this.

CORKER:
   Goin' on da plane! GOIN' ON DA PLANE!

FLORENCE:
   What does that mean?

GLENNY:
   It's a long story. Come on guy.

LEONARD:
   How'd he get way down here? Deep in the south end?

GLENNY:
There's no walls around it yet are there? I guess he just walked.

LEONARD:
But how would he find us?

GLENNY:
He probably followed you home after the funeral. He may have just hung around outside getting up the courage to knock.

LEONARD:
He didn't knock. He just walked in.

GLENNY:
Oh well. Not to worry. Corker's harmless. You've paid your last respects Cork. Time to go back.

CORKER:
(not moving) No Pit. NO PIT!

FLORENCE:
What's the Pit?

GLENNY:
That's what he calls the place where he lives.

CORKER:
Cantchain...cantchain....

FLORENCE:
What's he saying?

CORKER:
Goin' on da plane! GOIN' ON DA PLANE!

FLORENCE:
What does that mean?

MERIT:
Mother. Please just....

FLORENCE:
I want to know what does that means. He is Serena's friend. Going on a plane. What does that mean?

GLENNY:
His father left him at social services, didn't have the heart to say he wasn't coming back. When Cork asked the receptionist where he went, she didn't know what to say so she just said he was going away on a plane.

CORKER:
Goin' on da plane! Gonta heaven.

FLORENCE:
Dear God. He's all mixed up.

LEONARD:
Well this is all very sad but I think it's time that Mr. Glenny takes Corker back to where he belongs.

GLENNY:
Come on fella.

CORKER:
NO PIT!

FLORENCE:
He doesn't want to go.

MERIT:
Well he can't stay here! Please stay out of this mother!

FLORENCE:
What about the note?

GLENNY:
What note?

FLORENCE:
She gave him a note. It says: "Take care of Corker." We know what "take care" means. Or we used to.

MERIT:
This is ridiculous. It's not like inheriting a piano or a stray cat.

LEONARD:
It has no legal status, Florence.

FLORENCE:

You and your laws. It was her deathbed wish.

MERIT:

It was the last bad joke she played on me and I won't bite.
There are places for people like him. A whole system in
place for people like him. Our taxes pay for them. And it
isn't cheap. I'll handle this mother.

GLENNY listens with interest.

GLENNY:

Not to worry folks. Corker knows the score. Come on Cork.

CORKER backs away, shakes his head.

GLENNY:

(quietly) Sorry Cork. *(to LEONARD)* Grab his arms.

LEONARD:

What?

GLENNY:

Grab his arms!

*GLENNY, GAL and LEONARD take a hold of CORKER's arms. He
struggles.*

GLENNY:

Get a grip.

CORKER:

Goin' on da plane! No Pit! No Pit! No Pit!

MERIT:

Oh my God!

FLORENCE:

Don't hurt him.

*Furniture starts flying, vases of flowers overturned, ceramics hit
the floor.*

CORKER:

Gonta heaven! Gonta heaven! Cantchain!

MERIT:

Watch the table!

GAL:

Holy shit.

CORKER clears a table, knocks it over. His boots fly off. His feet are bare.

FLORENCE:

He has no socks.

GLENNY:

Hold his arms! Pin 'em man. Didn't you ever wrestle?

They finally get CORKER to the front door, chaos in his wake. For a moment he breaks free, then turns, facing into the room, his hands up against the doorframe, holding on for dear life. He remains frozen against the door frame in his bare feet.

GLENNY:

Tickle him.

MERIT:

(astounded) What?

GLENNY:

Corker's ticklish. Tickle him.

MERIT:

(hesitates) I will not!

GLENNY:

Do you want him out of here?

MERIT hesitates. For a moment, she is riveted by the terror in his eyes, then reaches out, tickles CORKER under the arm. His resistance immediately dissolves. He lets go of the door and they whisk him out.

CORKER:

(voice receding, weaker) No Pit. No Pit. No Pit.

FLORENCE and MERIT stand watching, shaken.

FLORENCE:

That's what you call handling it. Throwing poor souls out in the cold with no socks on.

MERIT:

I'm not responsible for his socks.

MERIT picks up CORKER's boots. GLENNY returns to pick them up.

MERIT:

He is.

GLENNY takes the boots and leaves. GAL and LEONARD re-enter, breathless.

GAL:

Strong little bugger isn't he? We better go pick up Margaret and the boys, head Up Home.

FLORENCE:

Do you want to carry me out too?

MERIT:

You need to get home and get some rest. We all need to regroup. Don't worry about this mom. I'll make some calls in the morning, make sure this is all sorted out. *(she kisses her)* I'll call you soon.

GAL and FLORENCE leave. LEONARD and MERIT survey the room. LEONARD starts cleaning.

LEONARD:

The week from hell.

MERIT:

Did you see the look in his eyes?

LEONARD:

I was too busy keeping his fists out of my face. Let's just leave everything. The cleaning lady can deal with this in the morning. And the insurance agent. Besides, it's past nine. You'd better get to bed. You'll need a pill. You've got a lot to deal with in the morning.

MERIT:
Yes.

LEONARD:
Go to bed and dream of gardenias and rum punches.

MERIT:
I'll try. *(MERIT turns off the lights)* No socks.

SCENE FOUR

Night. CORKER can be seen outside in the moonlight. He comes to the door of the solarium. He picks the lock, the door opens. He walks about the livingroom, picks up small things that interest him, puts them in his pocket. He pulls a little toy plastic boat from his coat and puts it in the water. He plays very quietly.

CORKER:
Bow in the wata. *(he floats it around, humming happily)*

He walks over to the piano then pulls it out into the middle of the room. He loves this piano. For him it isn't an eyesore. It's a treasure. He walks around it, studies it from various angles in the moonlit room. He sits down on the bench and plays a note. He begins to play a simple refrain, from 'Ode To Joy.' He begins to sing along. His words are quirky, sometimes almost indecipherable.

CORKER:
Li-en ta la melo-eeeee
A glaness sonig joe fal eee
Pla ah eh a spechal fen en….
A e ring tie en fall ee.

He stops, then he launches in to a much fuller version of 'Ode to Joy,' both hands, great intensity. He is a good piano player. He closes his eyes, enjoys the moment. The lights go on. LEONARD, astounded, stands in the doorway with a golf club in hand. CORKER just keeps on playing. MERIT staggers in, disoriented, a sleep mask pushed up on her forehead. She joins LEONARD in staring at him.

LEONARD:
  Tell me this isn't happening.

MERIT:
  Did the alarm go off?

LEONARD:
  We didn't set it.

  MERIT sits down, groggy.

MERIT:
  We didn't?

LEONARD:
  No we didn't!

MERIT:
  (half asleep) She used to play that. She must have taught him that. He's very good, isn't he?

  LEONARD claps his hands in front of MERIT's face.

LEONARD:
  Wake up!

  MERIT jolts awake.

LEONARD:
  (to CORKER) Hey! You! What the hell do you think you're doing!

  CORKER jumps up, scrambles onto the couch.

LEONARD:
  Call the police. Let them drag him out this time.

MERIT:
  No! Not the police.

LEONARD:
  We need a couple of big strong cops to get him out of here. My back can't take that again. Who are you calling?

MERIT:
  (going through phonebook) Social services.

CORKER:
  (muttering, whimpering in corner) Cantchain...cantchain....

LEONARD:
  At 4:30 in the morning.

MERIT:
  There's a 24-hour emergency number.... Hello hello!

LEONARD:
  Merit, we've been down that road.

  MERIT slams down the receiver.

MERIT:
  Leave a message! Doesn't anyone know what an emergency is anymore?

LEONARD:
  Yeah, the police.

MERIT:
  But he's not a criminal.

LEONARD:
  He broke into our house. He's trashing our furniture. This is all because of your goddamned sister. Here I thought there'd be one less MacPhee to put up with but no such luck.

  MERIT approaches CORKER.

MERIT:
  It's time to go. Could you please go now. Go on...out you go.

LEONARD:
  He's not a dog either.

MERIT:
  Please leave! It is very late and we should all be asleep. This is OUR house. Not your house. *(she points to the door)* Please go.

CORKER:
  (shakes his head) No Pit. No Pit!

LEONARD:

Call the police.

MERIT:

I'll sit up with him 'til we can get someone here.

LEONARD:

No way. I'm not leaving my wife all alone with a bum off the street in her nightie....

MERIT:

Glenny says he's harmless.

LEONARD:

Glenny is worse than useless is what Glenny is.

MERIT:

I'll sit up with him Leonard. You go back to bed. There's no point in us both losing sleep. *(to CORKER)* You go over there.

LEONARD:

This is nuts.

MERIT:

Go.

LEONARD turns and leaves. MERIT gets a cushion from the couch and the afghan and holds it out to CORKER. He grabs it and retreats to the corner. MERIT sinks into a chair, picks up the phone again.

SCENE FIVE

8:30 a.m. GLENNY's workspace. The radio is on. A warm activity room/work space; a computer, desk, filing cabinet stuffed in the corner but certainly not the focus of the room. A fridge, a toaster. There are a couple of barbells on the floor, a punching bag, board games, a table full of Lego constructions. A trunk. GLENNY looks like he has slept in his clothes. He is slumped over his desk, a pile of papers in front of him, on the phone.

GLENNY:

"You got the Maalox, the deodorants, the razor blades at
$4.59 a box...that's $9.80, two taxi stubs—$4.80 and $4.95
round trip to the doctor's, two boxes of diapers at $12.29....
They've gone up. Look, I don't have time for this. I've got
another 300 invoices to go through and you're nickel and
diming me on.... We got the Maalox, the deodorants, the
razor blades...the taxis, the diapers. They've gone up! That's
what I said. Adult diapers have gone up. They are not that
price anymore, no one can find them anywhere in the city
anymore for less than.... Value Fair has them on for.... How
the hell should I know? 'Cause they're bigger, they got more
material. They went up! Everything's gone up except the size
of the cheques...and the poor saps that are left on staff are
not willing to make up the difference any longer! D'you
understand! This has been three cheques in a row...you're
short changing us every goddamned month.

*MERIT storms in dressed in business suit, harried. CORKER
trailing. CORKER rushes over to the Lego table, starts working
furiously.*

MERIT:

He broke into our house at four in the morning.

GLENNY:

Gotta go. *(slams down the phone, looks over at CORKER)* Are you
okay Cork?

CORKER not looking up, nods his head furiously.

MERIT:

He broke into our house at four in the morning!

GLENNY:

I heard you the first time.

MERIT:

I've been sitting up with him for four hours calling a useless
so-called emergency line—every five minutes getting
nowhere and now I'm an hour late for a meeting! I want to
know how this happened?

GLENNY:

Corker's very good at picking locks.

MERIT:

You took him away. You said you would take care of things. What happened?

GLENNY:

I took him back to the Pit.

CORKER:

No Pit! No Pit!

GLENNY:

We watched 'Gilligan's Island.'

CORKER:

Ginger!

GLENNY:

Mary Ann! *(they do a high five)* Then I left. I guess he walked out after lights out.

MERIT:

He can walk out?

GLENNY:

It's not a prison. There are no locks on the door. The night staff can't be everywhere at once. They're overworked, tired out, understaffed. When things get bad for him in the Pit, he walks out and roams the streets.

CORKER:

No Pit! NO PIT!

GLENNY:

He used to end up at your sister's. That's the first place I'd look in the morning. He'd be sitting in the sun playing that piano.

MERIT:

Well find another piano. We don't want him in our house.

GLENNY turns to CORKER. CORKER has his eyes fixed on MERIT.

37

GLENNY:
Corker, do you hear the lady?

CORKER:
Laadee.

GLENNY:
The lady is upset. No more visits. No piano.

CORKER:
No piano.

MERIT:
Why does he keep staring at me? He's been doing that since four this morning.

GLENNY:
You remind him of her.

MERIT:
If he comes back again, we'll have no choice but to call the police. Does he know what that means?

GLENNY:
Oh yeah. Corker knows them all by name. Sometimes when things get bad for him in the Pit....

MERIT:
What do you mean when things get bad for him.... You keep saying that. Is there something wrong with the place?

GLENNY:
It's a temporary facility for people waiting for permanent placements.

MERIT:
Well if it's only temporary.

GLENNY:
'Cept he's been there for a year. He hates the noise. The snores, the wails, the radios.... His parents were old. Quiet. And there's a bully in the bunk next to him who makes his life miserable. He plays heavy metal, he calls him a retard. Puts frozen dog turds in his socks.

MERIT looks over at CORKER.

GLENNY:

Not very nice when they thaw out. It's given him a real bad association with socks. Bullies are a big problem, don't you think?

MERIT:

I have no idea. Why does he scratch his hand like that?

GLENNY:

Eczema.

MERIT:

Can't you get him into another place?

GLENNY:

He's been through them all. Nobody wants him back. He's no angel.

MERIT:

I thought you said he was harmless.

GLENNY:

Unless provoked. Then he's a wildman. How come you're the one who got stuck sitting up with him?

MERIT:

(looks at watch) I've got to go. I don't have any more time to deal with this. I'm already late for a meeting with the Premier.

GLENNY:

Tell him Albert Glenny says hello.

MERIT:

You know him?

GLENNY:

Sat next to him in grade ten. Claris Ferris. He got hounded something awful for that name. He'd do anything to get people to like him. And very impressionable. If he liked the colour of your sweatshirt he'd go right out and buy one at lunch. If he liked the place you had a hole in your jeans, he'd go home and saw a hole in his own—even if his mom just bought them. Very impressionable? Is he still like that?

MERIT just looks at him.

MERIT:
Don't change the subject. This can't happen again. What are you going to do about this?

GLENNY:
I'm getting him out of the Pit soon. Into Harbour House.

CORKER starts banging his Lego.

CORKER:
Habohowse!

MERIT:
What's that?

GLENNY:
A group home. A little one. A nice one. There's a piano. Cork'll be able to cook all he wants to. He loves to cook.

CORKER gets animated, listening to GLENNY talk about Harbour House. He starts banging the table in excitement.

CORKER:
Habahowse.

GLENNY:
I think I can get him in in a coupla months. We're just holding on, aren't we Corker?

CORKER:
Huldinon.

MERIT:
And the short term?

GLENNY:
I'll talk to him some more. It takes a while for things to sink in. We'll work it out.

MERIT:
Good. *(looks at watch)* Now I'm really late.

MERIT starts to leave. She can feel CORKER's eyes on her. She looks over at him, he turns his head down, works furiously at putting Lego pieces together.

CORKER:
(*blurts*) BYE!

MERIT:
(*hesitates*) Goodbye.

CORKER watches her go. GLENNY starts searching through a box of mitts and scarves.

GLENNY:
Let's find you some socks. Some socks you can trust. Trustworthy socks. (*GLENNY pulls out a pair of socks. Inspects them. CORKER grabs them from him, inspects them.*) Get 'em on and we'll go down and have a donut before workshop. I won the triactor last night. We'll get some chocolate bowties. Donuts on me for everyone for the next month.

CORKER:
BOWTIES!

They high five again.

CORKER:
Yes!

GLENNY:
No more splashing the water Cork. No more piano. I'll take you down to the Mall on the weekend, see the fountain there. 'Til then just THINK a piano, think a fountain. With all your might. (*GLENNY takes his fingers and taps the sides of his head*) Think think think think.

CORKER imitates him, tapping the sides of his own head with his fingers.

CORKER:
Thin thin thin thin....

GLENNY:
Think a fountain. That's the easiest. Costs nothing. Never disappointed. Fits in with the new world order.

CORKER:

Nuworlorer.

GLENNY:

Come on Cork. She's gonna do something for us Cork. I can feel it. That little hesitation towards the end. Hesitation. That's a good sign. There may be hope.

CORKER:

Hope.

GLENNY:

Come on.

CORKER grabs his hat and mitts. They leave.

SCENE SIX

The phone rings in MERIT and LEONARD's house. FLORENCE's voice is recorded on their machine in the empty house.

FLORENCE:

(message) Merit, this is your mother. I called you at 8:30 this morning, 6:30 at night and you're never there.

LEONARD walks into his house, carrying the mail. He makes no effort to pick up the phone.

FLORENCE:

(message) Where are you?

LEONARD:

Some meeting or other.

FLORENCE:

(message) Why have a home if you're never in it?

LEONARD:

Good question.

FLORENCE:

(message) Why not just sleep at the Y?

LEONARD:

They don't have rooms anymore.

FLORENCE:

(message) Who benefits from that lovely fountain? No one's around to even hear the water splashing on the rocks. When do you get home?

LEONARD:

In time to be flat out in the sack by nine o'clock. That's one thing we can be sure of in this world. And the bills coming in.

FLORENCE:

(message) Call me please. I don't have Serena's calls to look forward to anymore, and I would like….

> *FLORENCE's messages gets cut off. The phone rings. LEONARD makes no effort to answer it. Another message begins.*

CORKER:

(message) Hi! Hi! Reena! Gonta heaven.

LEONARD:

(staring at the phone) We give to the Sally Ann. We give to Christmas Daddies. United Appeal. I play basketball once a year for Big Brothers. I flip the odd buck to the guy panhandling out front the office. I am not a bad person.

CORKER:

(message) Goin' on da plane! GOIN' ON DA PLANE!

LEONARD:

(picks up the phone) Quit calling us! Leave us alone. Please! *(slams down the phone)*

SCENE SEVEN

Black. Night. MERIT and LEONARD's house. CORKER is back outside the garden door. He picks the locks, opens the door. As soon as he is inside, the lights go on, the alarm goes off. CORKER panics, covers his ears, starts howling, cowering in a corner. MERIT enters, golf club in hand, incredulous. LEONARD staggers in after her.

LEONARD:
  What the....

MERIT:
  Turn it off.

  LEONARD goes to the key pad, punches buttons frantically. Nothing happens.

MERIT:
  What are you doing?

LEONARD:
  I...don't remember how.

MERIT:
  You set it!

LEONARD:
  Yeah, well I can't unset it!

MERIT:
  Oh for God's sakes.

  MERIT goes over to the keypad, punches it a couple of times, until it goes off. LEONARD grabs the golf club from her hand and moves towards CORKER threateningly, brandishing his golf club. CORKER jumps back onto the couch.

LEONARD:
  Get out of my house!

  LEONARD raises the club. MERIT takes LEONARD's arm and tries to pull it down. They struggle.

MERIT:
Leonard don't....

*CORKER lets out a loud wail and springs on LEONARD's back.
LEONARD astounded, throws him off. CORKER jumps to his feet,
starts circling, threateningly.*

LEONARD:
(shaken) Call the police.

MERIT goes to the phone.

SCENE EIGHT

*GLENNY is studying a race form, on the phone, laying bets on
horses.*

GLENNY:
I want Lucky Lady to win, Harry's Bad Day to show....

MERIT storms in, looking really wrecked.

MERIT:
He did it again.

GLENNY:
Where is he?

MERIT:
We had to call the police. He attacked my husband. It took
them an hour to get there and then it was the same bloody
thing all over again. He almost ripped the door frame off
this time. Police cars, flashing lights...who knows what the
neighbours thought. God, I feel like I've been punched.

*GLENNY shoves a chair over towards her. MERIT sits. GLENNY
paces.*

GLENNY:
Did you charge him?

MERIT:
(miserable) No. We didn't charge him.

GLENNY:

It's not like Corker to attack someone unless…did you provoke him?

MERIT:

My husband was trying to get him to leave.

GLENNY:

What happened? I'll have to file a report on this.

MERIT:

Well…he broke in. The alarm went off. He jumped up on the couch with his big muddy boots. My husband sort of swung his golf club around in the air to get him to leave. I tried to pull Leonard's arm down. He pushed me then Corker attacked….

GLENNY:

He was trying to protect you.

MERIT:

Oh please! What are you going to do about this? What is your next course of action? Obviously talking doesn't work.

GLENNY:

He was trying to protect you!

MERIT:

I don't need protection! I need my sleep! I have a very stressful job and I can't have people breaking into my house in the middle of the night. I have to have my wits about me.

GLENNY:

They've probably drugged him, grounded him. Poor bugger. That's the low maintenance solution at the Pit. Drug them and let them stare at the walls. Cheaper than counselling or programs. And there's more coming, isn't there? I better get over there.

MERIT:

More what?

GLENNY:
More cuts. We'll get the news just before the Premier and his cronies go off on their winter vacations. Am I right? Am I right? Cut cut cut. That's the only tune he knows.

MERIT:
First I have my house broken into and then I have to listen to one of your rants about the Premier.

GLENNY:
Cut welfare, cut social services, cut education, but he doesn't touch the corporations and the bond dealers. He's sucking up to them just like he sucked up to the guys with the best looking cars in high school. Am I right?

MERIT:
Would you please just start taking some responsibility for Mr. Cork?

GLENNY:
Isn't that what your sister asked you to do?

MERIT:
Corker is not my responsibility! He's yours. But since you can't handle it I'll make sure someone else does!

GLENNY:
Good! Great! Halleluljah! Help is on the way Cork!

MERIT storms out.

SCENE NINE

MERIT and LEONARD's house. A week later. MERIT and LEONARD enter, dragging themselves in, throw everything down. LEONARD flops down on couch. MERIT turns on the answering machine, then drops down beside him.

CORKER:
(*message*) Reena! Reena. Gonnnnda heeeaaaven. Goooinnnn' on da plane. Hi!

FLORENCE:

    (message) It's your mother. I'm taking the bus down to have dinner with you.

GAL:

    (message) Merit, I need to talk to you. I know we said after Serena's funeral that we could wait to talk until next month but I can't....

CORKER:

    (message) Goin' on da plane. Gonta heaven. GONTA HEAVEN!

FLORENCE:

    (message) It's your mother again. You're never home. All I ever do is talk to this machine. Why don't you just turn off the machine, stay home and listen to your waterfall.

    LEONARD jumps up, goes over to the wall and pulls the jack right out of the wall.

MERIT:

    (incredulous) What are you doing?

LEONARD:

    She's right. Let's just turn off the phone, climb down from the world, and listen to our expensive fountain splashing onto our expensive rocks.

    LEONARD starts pacing in small circles, disconnected phone in hand.

LEONARD:

    I feel like a rat on a wheel.

MERIT:

    What's the matter with you?

LEONARD:

    I've lost control...even in my own house. It's not enough that I haven't had a decent fucking piece of work in five months, I'm being harassed by a plague of mentals and MacPhees in the sanctity of my own home.

MERIT:

It'll be alright.

LEONARD:

No, it won't.

MERIT:

I'm going to handle this.

LEONARD:

(interrupts) Well you haven't! He's still with us, isn't he? Calling us up a hundred times a day. Doesn't look like you're handling it to me!

MERIT:

I talked to the head of the Department. It's not that simple.

LEONARD:

Obviously not.

MERIT:

Glenny works with all the hard cases that no one else wants. He's old style, abrasive, not a team player but he works his ass off. If they lose Glenny, they might as well just turn off the lights and let everyone run wild in the streets.

LEONARD:

Isn't that what's happening now?

MERIT:

He's trying to get Corker into Harbour House sooner.

LEONARD:

Today.

MERIT:

No. Not today.

LEONARD:

When?

MERIT:

Sooner.

LEONARD:

What does that mean?

MERIT:

Sooner. Sooner than if I hadn't asked. What the hell are you doing?

LEONARD:

I'd like to help that guy too but I can't. *(grabs a handful of bills from the desk)* I'm an acquisitions lawyer and no one's acquiring. I'm getting treated like the coffee boy by my partners 'cause I'm not producing. I gotta steel myself when I go in there so that I can get through the day. That's where I'm putting my energies. There's a lot of sad, bloody cases out there and, unfortunately, your husband is one of them!

MERIT:

Stop it!

LEONARD moves the piano as close to the wall as possible.

LEONARD:

And what about this? Why the hell is it still here? We live in a half million dollar house and the centrepiece in the livingroom is a piano so beat up the Sally Ann won't take it.

MERIT:

I'll get rid of it before you get back. *(changing subject)* What time is your flight tomorrow?

LEONARD:

Eight.

MERIT:

I never asked where you're going.

LEONARD:

Toronto.

MERIT:

What for?

LEONARD:

A trade fair.

MERIT:

(tries to be encouraging) That sounds interesting.

LEONARD:
 If you're selling motor homes. Who ever thought lawfirms would be peddling their wares that way? Do you think my father went to trade fairs to keep his practice afloat?

MERIT:
 Who else is going?

LEONARD:
 Charles and Richard. I think they've set up some meetings. They're just taking me along to fill up a seat at the conference table.

MERIT:
 Let's have dinner together.

LEONARD:
 There's some cold chicken in the fridge. I'm going back to the office.

MERIT:
 Do you have to? You'll be gone five days.

LEONARD:
 I won't be too late. Get some sleep.

 LEONARD goes by without touching her.

MERIT:
 Leonard? *(he stops)* Six days 'til Costa Rica.

SCENE TEN

 Night. CORKER approaches the garden door, jimmies the lock, opens the door. The alarm goes off. He walks in. Suddenly, he cries out in pain, begins jumping about, turns and runs out into the darkness. LEONARD arrives, golfclub in hand, looks around the floor, satisfied. MERIT follows. LEONARD goes to the alarm keypad, turns off the alarm.

LEONARD:
 Worked like a charm.

MERIT:

What did?

LEONARD:

I put down some rat traps from the cottage. I thought we needed another disincentive to keep the intrepid Corker out.

MERIT:

But rat traps!

LEONARD:

Do you want to go through this every night? We had to discourage him. Reason doesn't work. The social services don't work. I had to do something to protect my home and my wife while I'm away. I'd say that's the end of it.

MERIT picks up CORKER's bright yellow toque which he left behind, turns it over in her hand.

SCENE ELEVEN

MERIT enters GLENNY's office, toque in hand. CORKER is sitting in the corner playing Lego. He huddles down when he sees her.

MERIT:

Here's his hat.

GLENNY takes the hat, coldly, turns back to his work. MERIT looks over at CORKER.

MERIT:

(hesitates) Is he all right?

GLENNY:

He's got bruised feet.

MERIT:

He can't break into our house....

GLENNY:

So you set rat traps for him. He's got enough troubles
without south end lawyers setting rat traps for him. Bullies.
They're everywhere.

MERIT:

He's calling fifty times a day. He's breaking in every night.
You've got to do something.

GLENNY:

What can I do? I'm not a jailer. I'm not a magician. I'm just a
lowly social worker with 135 other Corkers in my caseload.
What the hell do you want me to do? What have you got in
mind? If a man wants something so badly that he'll rip off
door frames and risk the wrath of lawyers swinging golfclubs,
what can I do?

MERIT:

(looks over at CORKER) What...does he want?

GLENNY:

He wants you. He was loyal to your sister and now he's loyal
to you. You understand loyalty. It's like you and your
Premier. You keep the faith. You don't question. You're at
his beck and call. When he says jump, you say how high?
That's the main qualification for the job. It doesn't matter
how worthy the subject of the loyalty is. And it doesn't with
Corker either. In his eyes, you can do no wrong. You have
inherited Corker's loyalty.

MERIT is stunned by this.

MERIT:

(finally) I don't want it.

GLENNY:

Then get a court order. Maybe the police can keep him away.

MERIT:

Maybe?

GLENNY:

They can't watch him twenty-four hours a day unless they put him in jail. For that, you'd have to charge him with something. Break and enter. Harassment.

MERIT just stares over at CORKER putting his Lego together.

GLENNY:

'Course that would screw up his chances of getting into Harbour House. He'd end up in the back ward of the hospital banging his head against the wall for all eternity.

MERIT:

(after a pause) What should I do, Glenny?

GLENNY:

Let him in.

MERIT:

What?

GLENNY:

Let him in. He's lonely. He misses your sister. In a while he'll get used to the fact that she's gone, then he'll get into Harbour House and he won't need you anymore. Just...let him in.

SCENE TWELVE

MERIT and LEONARD's house. The front door opens. MERIT enters, followed by GAL and FLORENCE. CORKER stands at the doorway holding a bunch of pizza boxes but he will not enter.

MERIT:

Don't stop. What are you stopping for? It's okay to come in. Come on. Come! Nothing will hurt you. Here, I'll take those pizza boxes.

CORKER holds onto the pizza boxes tightly. He won't move.

GAL:

If he's in you can't get him out. If he's out, you can't get him in.

54

MERIT:
Come in!

CORKER won't budge.

CORKER:
Man.

MERIT:
Man?

CORKER:
No man! NO MAN!

MERIT:
Man? *(she realizes he means LEONARD)* No man! Man's gone on the plane.

GAL:
What are you talking about?

MERIT:
He means Leonard. No man. Man's gone on the plane. Gone! Man gone.

CORKER:
Gone?

MERIT:
Gone. Man gone. Come in.

CORKER cautiously enters.

GAL:
What's he got against Leonard?

MERIT:
Never mind. *(to CORKER)* I'll take the pizza into the kitchen and cut it up, put in onto plates.

CORKER will not give up the pizza boxes.

MERIT:
Just for a minute.

CORKER shakes his head, holds on firmly to boxes.

FLORENCE:
Just bring the plates in. We'll stay here and guard the pizza.

MERIT:
Alright.

GAL:
I'll help.

MERIT heads for the kitchen. GAL follows. FLORENCE walks over to the fountain, holds her hand out to the water.

FLORENCE:
Do you miss Serena?

CORKER:
Reena.

FLORENCE:
Sometimes, I wake up in the morning and I've forgotten that she's gone And then the fog starts to clear in my brain and it comes back to me—and it's like a big scar on the horizon. She died too young. She was sick. It was a terrible disease. It came upon her very quickly. Have you ever heard of flesh eating disease? It was sort of like that. Similar. I saw her two days before and then….

FLORENCE takes a picture out of her purse.

FLORENCE:
This is the three of them when they were little. Aren't they beautiful? I loved their names. They were filled with such promise. Serena. Galahad. Merit. They were happy children. Look at those faces. Happy. Smiling. Happy together they were. Like three little puppies, the way they tumbled around. I love this picture. *(CORKER comes over and looks down at it.)*

CORKER:
Happy.

FLORENCE:
Sure there were problems; Serena had her…problems. We all had to try and deal with them. Merit was a worrier. Even back then. And then she hooked up with Leonard and it got

a hundred times worse. She's got those awful headaches. I bet she worries twenty-four hours a day. She never smiles when she's with him. He's turned her into a watchchecker. I don't see any warmth, and no kissing.

CORKER:
No kissin'.

FLORENCE :
And Gal's all shagged up. I hear him and Margaret fighting at night after the kids are in bed. About money. But what can I do? Where do I fit in it all? I don't. One day I was the mother of three beautiful children. I was the mayor's wife. I was invited out five times a week—to luncheons, to teas. I had status—sort of—I certainly had a lot of hats—And in the wink of an eye, I'm seventy-five, I'm under attack from hockey pucks fired at my door and my son's wife is treating me like a child for putting my used tea bags in cups in the cupboard. Things change so quickly. Let's try to make this place a bit more lived in, shall we?

> *FLORENCE picks up a decorator pillow from a chair and pitches it across the room. CORKER finally drops the pizza boxes and starts helping her. CORKER picks up a little pewter boat and puts it in his pocket.*

SCENE THIRTEEN

> *The kitchen. MERIT is getting plates, cutting up vegetables.*

GAL:
I need to talk.

MERIT:
How is she doing? Is she still in denial?

GAL:
She told the mailman Serena was killed instantly by a falling flowerpot.

MERIT:

I guess it doesn't matter, really. It's behind us now. Time to look ahead. But you've got to watch for depression. Depression in seniors is very common. Vitamins are important. It's good she's got the kids to entertain her. Does she still play bridge with Ruth McGinnis?

GAL:

No.

MERIT:

Why not?

GAL:

Ruth died two years ago.

MERIT:

I didn't know that, did I?

GAL:

You sent a big jeezly bouquet to the funeral home. It was the biggest one there.

MERIT:

God. Sometimes it's all just such a blur. I have the most incredible headache. Pass me the serviettes. Is she still going to church?

GAL:

Yes.

MERIT:

Do you still take her out for Sunday drives?

GAL:

Sometimes.

MERIT:

She needs routines that she can count on.

GAL:

Can we please talk!

MERIT:

All right.

GAL takes a deep breath.

GAL:

The company has been struggling for quite a while.

MERIT:

Well it's never easy starting a new....

GAL:

(cuts her off) I did all the right things this time. I took your advice and I went to the self-confidence workshop. I worked on my attitude. I was upbeat. I was energized. Wasn't I?

MERIT:

Yes, you seemed pretty....

GAL:

And I did the market studies. Just like you said, didn't I? Didn't I?

MERIT:

What does this....

GAL:

I took the small business courses, I invested in the technology. I surrounded myself with winners. I did the whole business plan thing. I worked sixty hours a week. So did Margaret. I did all the right things. But sea cucumbers aren't moving.

MERIT:

They're not?

GAL:

Nope.

MERIT:

Well these things take time.

GAL:

And Economic Renewal has cancelled the program for small crustacean exports. They're focusing on arts and crafts this year. There is no more time.

MERIT:

What are you saying?

GAL:

To put it bluntly, the arse is out of her. The company's gone tits up.

MERIT:

Well, that's…unfortunate.

GAL:

You're not kidding.

MERIT:

But you'll just have to learn from your mistakes and move on. Let's have some pizza.

GAL:

There's more.

MERIT:

What do you mean?

GAL:

I'm in a bit of a jam.

MERIT:

(dread) What kind of a jam?

GAL:

I mortgaged the house to finance the business.

MERIT:

(astounded) What?

GAL:

I had to come up with collateral at the front end…. I thought it was a sure thing. You have to take risks. That's what they said at the workshop. That's what all the books say. You've said that yourself. You have to spend money to make money.

MERIT:

Your own money Gal. Not your mother's, not your sister's.
First you ran the family business into the ground. Then you
sold off the orchard.

GAL:

No one ever used the orchard anymore. You never come
home. The kids are too busy playing hockey. It was stupid to
have all that space just sitting there.

MERIT:

You have no sense Gal. That's the family home. Does she
know?

GAL:

I didn't want to worry her.

MERIT:

(in shock) What were you thinking? What if it all fell through?

GAL:

Well I didn't think it would…. You have to think positive.
That's what I did. I was very positive.

MERIT:

How bad is it?

GAL:

If we don't start paying a thousand a month, the bank will
offload it. And it will be torn down to make an overflow
parking lot for the donut shop.

MERIT:

When do you have to start paying?

GAL:

Yesterday. But I can put them off 'til May.

MERIT:

(holds her head) God, my head….

GAL:

Are you alright?

MERIT:

It feels like it's going to split in half. Then everything inside will just drip out all over the floor.

GAL:

You should see about those headaches. That doesn't sound good to me.

MERIT:

No.

GAL:

I need some help Merit.

MERIT:

Not now.

GAL:

Well then when?

MERIT:

After Year End. I'll talk to Leonard. I'll let you know when you're here for Easter dinner.

SCENE FOURTEEN

Later. The place looks very lived in. CORKER is sitting on the floor devouring the last little piece of cheese from around the rim of a pizza box. MERIT has a cloth on her forehead in an effort to ease her head.

GAL:

Well he sure liked that.

CORKER lets out a huge burp.

CORKER:

Rude! No burping. RUDE!

GAL:

That's right. Rude. I'm going outside for a smoke.

FLORENCE is watching her daughter.

FLORENCE:
I read an article about teeth grinding. It's caused by stress. Do you still grind your teeth?

MERIT:
I don't think so. My dentist hasn't mentioned it.

FLORENCE :
What do you do to get rid of your stress?

MERIT:
Oh I don't know mother…. I guess I…drink lots of coffee. And I clean.

MERIT jumps up, starts straightening. FLORENCE watches. So does CORKER.

MERIT:
There used to be a pewter turtle right there. Right there.

FLORENCE:
Serena didn't have stress.

MERIT:
She just caused it in others.

FLORENCE:
I think she wanted children. Funny, I had two daughters and neither of them have children. Thank heavens for Gal. It didn't take him long to start procreating.

MERIT:
No, that's one thing he's good at. And a jade bird that sat right beside it. There are things missing from this house.

FLORENCE:
Do you and Leonard ever just sit and hold hands and just listen to the sound of the water?

MERIT:
No.

FLORENCE:
Your father and I were going to Portugal the day he retired. We were both really looking forward to it. There was the big

reception in the town offices. They gave me my new suitcases. I slipped out to buy some of those little travel soaps and when I came back, he'd had the stroke. And then he lay there like a basket case for five years. Who knows? Maybe he travelled in his mind. I know I did. You have to gather the rosebuds while you can.

MERIT:

Costa Rica. That's where we gather rosebuds. I'm going to just go into the kitchen now and clean up....

FLORENCE:

I'll do it. You have a visitor. Serena's friend. It's only polite that you entertain him.

MERIT and CORKER are left in the livingroom. CORKER stares at her.

MERIT:

Would you like to play the piano?

CORKER:

Yano.

MERIT:

Go ahead.

CORKER sits down at the piano, plays a song.

MERIT:

I haven't heard that in.... She taught you that, didn't she? It's almost like.... We really weren't at all alike. She was the dreamer. I was the nuts and bolts. She was funny, crazy, emotional, irresponsible. She had these mood swings that got worse and worse as she got older.... She could be so charming and generous and bright that you just felt like a dull penny when you were with her...and then she could change in a flash. Like lightning. It was stunning really. It was terrifying.

She watches CORKER play.

MERIT:

You know what my father said about me? He said: "With any luck, Merit can get a job with the civil service, fade into the woodwork 'til it was time to draw a pension." I never inspired celestial images. But I didn't fade into the woodwork. The Premier has promised me Clerk of the Cabinet if I get the numbers down in this budget. What do you see when you look at me?

GAL re-enters.

GAL:

It's getting late. We'd better head out.

CORKER tenses.

MERIT:

That was the deal, Corker. I've got something for you. Get your boots on, get ready to go.

MERIT exits. CORKER holds on to the piano.

GAL:

I know how you feel guy. I'm just one step away from holding a tin cup myself. Don't expect much from her. She couldn't wait to leave us all behind, jump to the big time. Down to the city, to the south end. Never see her except for their family dinners twice a year. Thanksgiving and Easter. Perfectly spaced. No presents required. Kids trash the place. Leonard parades around in an apron making strange foods. Merit treats us all like creatures from outer space. She painted Serena right out of the picture. Never saw her for the last five years 'til the day of the funeral…and you know, I don't even think she looked into the coffin. Just walked right by talking on her cell phone. But there's one thing I do know—I hate that fountain, always makes me have to take a piss. *(GAL exits)*

CORKER:

No pissin'.

CORKER picks up a marble ashtray, inspects it, then puts it in his pocket. MERIT and FLORENCE enter.

MERIT:
Here's a care package for you from the fruit and vegetable store. Something other than donuts. Look. Kiwi, grapes, bananas.

CORKER starts popping grapes.

MERIT:
Wait 'til you get home.

GAL returns.

GAL:
Let's go. We'll drive you back to the Pit.

CORKER tenses.

FLORENCE:
We'll sit in the back together.

MERIT:
That was the deal Corker. If you behave yourself, you can come again.

CORKER puts on his coat. He rushes over and kisses MERIT on the cheek. She is stunned.

CORKER:
Bye.

CORKER leaves. MERIT closes the door after them. She puts her hand up to where he'd kissed her. She looks around the empty room, sits down to a stack of work, humming the song CORKER was playing on the piano.

SCENE FIFTEEN

Hours later. CORKER comes up to the outside door. The light catches his hair. He sits down on his heels, opens his bag of fruit, begins eating. He is guarding over her now. Inside, MERIT is sitting at her desk surrounded by a little pool of light. She looks at her watch, takes off her reading glasses, stretches. She reaches over and turns out the light.

SCENE SIXTEEN

Three days later. CORKER is shovelling snow outside the front window. LEONARD stares at him then enters with his suitcases. He is in a very good mood. MERIT enters with a couple of suitcases of her own, is startled to see him.

MERIT:
You're not due 'til tonight!

LEONARD:
I caught an earlier flight.

MERIT:
Don't say a thing. I'm looking after the piano right this minute. *(she starts looking through the phone book)* I cleared my desk, I picked up the tickets and the passports. I was just about to go through the yellow pages and see if I could find a taker....

LEONARD:
(dismisses it) We can deal with it when we get home.

MERIT:
(surprised) We can?

LEONARD:
No problem.

MERIT:
You're wondering what Corker's doing here.

LEONARD:
Looks like he's shovelling the walk.

MERIT:
We were using the wrong tactic. I had him over for pizza with mother and Gal. Killed three birds with one stone. Now I've got him doing odd jobs like shovelling the walks and there's no more nocturnal visits. I came up with a low maintenance solution.

LEONARD puts his arms around her, kisses her.

LEONARD:

Impressive. Good girl.

MERIT:

Why are you so cheerful all of a sudden?

LEONARD:

Slamemshut International.

MERIT:

What about them?

LEONARD:

You've heard of them.

MERIT:

Of course. Medical management, long term care....

LEONARD:

You're going to hear a lot more about them.

MERIT:

Why?

LEONARD:

That's who we met with. They're moving into this area and we're representing them.

MERIT:

Leonard!

LEONARD:

They wanted a company familiar with the territory. Who better than us? And I'm going to be chief counsel. They went through everyone at the firm and they chose me.

MERIT:

They did?

LEONARD:

They want to make a proposal to the province late spring.

MERIT:

The province?

LEONARD:

Who's the biggest provider of health services?

MERIT:

Well the province but…I mean if you're representing them and I'm working for….

LEONARD starts kissing her.

LEONARD:

Let's fall off that bridge when we come to it, shall we?

MERIT:

What are you doing?

LEONARD:

I just noticed how great you look. And you smell delicious.

MERIT:

I do?

LEONARD:

Why don't we just go upstairs and start our holiday a bit early.

MERIT:

It's the middle of the day.

LEONARD:

So?

MERIT:

We haven't done that in…I can't remember….

LEONARD:

Loosen up.

MERIT:

I have to finish packing. I have to call the papers and cancel our subscriptions.

LEONARD:

I'll call the papers. You do whatever you have to do. We'll rendezvous upstairs in five minutes.

MERIT:

Well I guess….*(smiles, shrugs)* Why not?

LEONARD slaps her playfully on the rear end. She exits.
LEONARD goes to the phone.

LEONARD:
  Yeah, give me the number for the Daily News please.

  *LEONARD waits. CORKER comes in the garden door, shovel in
  hand. He looks around. He sees the suitcases sitting at the front
  door.*

LEONARD:
  (writes number down on paper, then makes another call)
  Circulation department please. *(singing to himself)* Going on a
  plane. Gonna have some fun! Drinking margaritas...sitting
  in the sun. We're buggering off! Yes!

  LEONARD starts doing the Macarena.

LEONARD:
  Yeah, hi, I'd like to have our newspapers held for ten days
  please. Leonard Mills...1282 Edgehill Road. Starting
  again...April 1. Okeedokee.

  *CORKER sees the tickets and passports, picks them up, tries to fit
  them into his pocket but they won't fit. He panics, drops them into
  the guts of the piano. LEONARD turns, startled.*

LEONARD:
  Yikes! Don't scare me like that! You gotta learn some basic
  rules. Like knocking. Here, watch this.

  LEONARD goes over to the glass door, knocks on it loudly.

LEONARD:
  See. Like that. Try it.

  CORKER goes over and knocks loudly on the door.

LEONARD:
  You got it. Life's a lot easier if you learn some basic rules.

  CORKER doesn't move.

LEONARD:
  Did she forget to pay you?

LEONARD pulls out his wallet, holds a fiver to CORKER, then puts it back, gives him a twenty instead.

LEONARD:
  What the hell. Take it easy fella.

  CORKER takes the money and leaves.

SCENE SEVENTEEN

Darkness. CORKER is outside the garden doors in the moonlight. He puts his hand up in a flying motion.

CORKER:
  Goin' on da plane. Goin' on da plane….

SCENE EIGHTEEN

MERIT and LEONARD, dressed in tourist clothes are tearing the place apart looking for their tickets and passports.

MERIT:
  They were sitting right there on the fountain. I showed them to you then I went upstairs….

LEONARD:
  Are you sure you didn't take them upstairs?

MERIT:
  No.

LEONARD:
  You didn't leave them somewhere.

MERIT:
  No I didn't!

LEONARD:
  You were nuts to let that guy back into the house.

MERIT:
  We'll get them back.

LEONARD:

The plane is leaving in three quarters of an hour. We're never going to make it.

MERIT:

The cab's waiting. We'll get there.

The doorbell rings. LEONARD goes to the door, lets in GLENNY leading CORKER grudgingly.

MERIT:

Where are they? Where did you put the tickets?

CORKER:

Ticas.

GLENNY:

Easy! You don't know he took them.

MERIT:

He took them. Where are they?

CORKER:

Where?

GLENNY:

I checked his room. Checked the Pit. No passports, no tickets.

MERIT:

(Right in his face) Tell me where they are!

GLENNY:

Don't yell at him!

CORKER:

(distraught) Goin' on da plane. Gonta heaven. Reena.

MERIT:

Where are those tickets!

CORKER hangs his head in dejection.

LEONARD:

The plane is leaving in less than an hour.

MERIT:

Do you know what this trip means to me? I look forward to
this trip all year. I count the days. I live for this trip! Where
did you put them?

CORKER:

Where?

MERIT:

I've sat up with you all night. I've given you pizza, we gave
you work and we won't put up with this garbage!

*MERIT circles around, starts frantically going through the papers
on the desk one more time.*

CORKER:

Garbage.

LEONARD:

D'you hear that? He said garbage. I'll check the garbage
outside. Maybe he dropped the tickets in the garbage on his
way out. You check that one.

*LEONARD exits. MERIT starts rummaging through the garbage by
the desk.*

GLENNY:

I guess he doesn't want you to go. He'd miss you. He's grown
attached to you. Your winning ways.

MERIT:

I need this holiday. I need it.

GLENNY:

Of course you do. You need a holiday from your life.

MERIT:

I love my life!

LEONARD:

(Returning) They're not there.. We're not going to make it!

MERIT:

(MERIT grabs CORKER's collar menacingly) Where are they? So
help me, if you screw up this holiday....

CORKER:

Goin' on da plane! Cantchain! Cantchain.

CORKER frightened, shakes his head.

MERIT:

Shut up! I'm sick of your jibberish!

GLENNY:

Behold…the voice of reason.

MERIT:

Where are they?

GLENNY:

The calm, even-handed civil servant, out to serve the public good.

LEONARD:

Who the hell do you think you are coming in here with your smart mouth. Some low-grade thug with a chintzy community college certificate!

GLENNY:

At least I don't set rattraps for people!

LEONARD swings at him.

GLENNY:

Come and get me!

LEONARD and GLENNY start circling, fists ready.

MERIT:

Stop it!

CORKER:

(distressed, jumping around) Yano! Yano!

MERIT:

What?

CORKER goes to the piano, and fishes the tickets and the passports out.

MERIT:

Leonard look!

LEONARD drops his fists, grabs the tickets from CORKER's hand. MERIT and LEONARD collect up their things. She looks at CORKER who stands frightened, stranded by the piano.

LEONARD:
Now get the hell out of here and don't come back! I'll set the alarm.

CORKER doesn't want to go.

LEONARD:
Get out. GET OUT!

GLENNY:
Come on Cork.

He just keeps staring at MERIT.

MERIT:
Just go. Please.

CORKER turns and leaves. GLENNY follows. MERIT, shaken, watches after them. LEONARD sets the alarm, picks up his bags.

LEONARD:
We're off.

MERIT leaves. LEONARD closes the door after her.

SCENE NINETEEN

Lights up on CORKER in a pool of light. Lost. Alone.

CORKER:
Goin' on da plane. Gonta heaven.

ACT TWO

SCENE ONE

Easter Sunday. MERIT is standing in the middle of the livingroom. Tanned, beautifully dressed but still tense. The piano is still there. She straightens a picture on the wall, picks up some fluff off the floor, sits down, opens a magazine. LEONARD comes in from the kitchen wearing an apron. He sits down in a chair, nose in a cookbook.

MERIT:
(jumps) I never know what to do on Easter Sunday. I feel so...indulgent.

LEONARD:
I feel the exact opposite.

MERIT:
What are you looking up?

LEONARD:
Potato blossoms. Your mother loved them the last time I made them.

MERIT:
That's nice.

MERIT walks over to the couch which CORKER had climbed on with his muddy boots. She brushes at it.

MERIT:
They didn't quite get the footprints out.

MERIT brushes some more, looks down critically, finally throws a pillow over it. She looks at LEONARD, hesitates, then launches in.

MERIT:
We're very lucky aren't we?

LEONARD:
Lucky?

MERIT:

I'm Clerk of the Cabinet now. You've got the big contract.
We're lucky to have such exciting, challenging work.

LEONARD:

I don't think luck has much to do with it. I'd say tenacity and
hard work.

MERIT:

Well yes, but it's at a time when there's such hardship—
generally.

LEONARD:

We've had our share. Last month, the Corker fiasco. The
next three hours I'm going to have to endure your family.
What time are they coming?

MERIT:

Four. The children can run around outside for an hour. Get
everyone seated by six. Finished by seven o'clock. Coffee,
dessert, a bit more time outside. Play on the computer. With
luck, they'll be out the door by seven thirty.

LEONARD:

Sounds good to me. *(starts to get up)* Better get at it then.

MERIT:

Leonard? Gal's got himself in another mess. His latest
business has gone belly up. He used the house as collateral
and now the bank owns it. Someone has to start making
payments or it's gone.

LEONARD:

Someone?

MERIT:

Us.

LEONARD:

Well I assume you told him to piss up a rope.

MERIT:

I told him I would talk to you about it.

LEONARD:

Well thanks for telling me an hour before they arrive.

MERIT:

I'm sorry.

LEONARD:

We've just spent two weeks in Costa Rica. You could have mentioned it there.

MERIT:

We don't take our troubles to Costa Rica. That's our rule. We focus on rum punches and perfecting our tans.

LEONARD:

Except you didn't. You moped around like you had the weight of the world on your shoulders. We might as well have stayed home.

MERIT:

I'm sorry.

LEONARD:

He wants you to start paying mortgage payments on a house you haven't lived in in twenty years. When were you there last? A year ago? Two years ago? For a day. Not even overnight because you don't like to see how his kids have trashed the place. And he wants us to make payments on it? That's crazy, isn't it? Isn't it?

MERIT:

Well, I guess so but we have tossed around the idea of retiring up there someday. There's lots of space to build a little place at the back.

LEONARD:

And a donut shop next door. Hardly idyllic.

MERIT:

We could put up a big fence.

LEONARD:

We'd still smell the donuts and the exhaust from the cars. Not my idea of fun. And by the time we retire, the hospital will probably be long gone—with all the cuts. I'm not going into my decrepitude in a sleepy little town without any healthcare facilities. It's not the booming metropolis it was when your father was mayor. The more I think about it, the more I think he's got his bloody nerve even asking us. I know it's hard for you to think clearly when it comes to your family but....

MERIT:
Oh don't lecture me! Maybe that's why I didn't raise it sooner. 'Cause I knew you'd get like this!

LEONARD:
Like what?

MERIT:
All puffed up, huffy....

LEONARD:
Well I'm sorry. But someone's got to point out some economic realities. And speaking of houses, what about this house? It needs painting. We need a new furnace. Our insurance premiums are going through the roof thanks to Corker. The trip cost us more than we budgeted and we enjoyed it less! *(gestures towards fountain)* All that business over there just about broke the bank.

MERIT:
We have the money Leonard.

LEONARD:
But for how long?

MERIT:
Well....

LEONARD:
You've got the big job now but for how long? One year? Two. Governments come and go. One minute you're hot, the next minute you can have about as much cachet as cold cannelloni.

MERIT:
Oh come on.

LEONARD:

You said yesterday that Gilbert is trying to reposition himself.
He's not just standing still. You've got to keep an eye on
Gilbert. 'Cause Gilbert is sure keeping an eye on you.
Waiting for one false move. Nothing is secure these days, is
it? Your brother doesn't understand that. He just sees big
house, big car, big jobs…but he doesn't know how
precarious it all is.

MERIT:

Well he has gone bankrupt twice. I guess he does know
how….

LEONARD:

But he never plans. He never thinks more that one day
ahead. Your whole family's like that. Even your father was
like that. Big generous mayor, throwing money around like
there was no tomorrow, leaving a big debt in his wake. And
Gal's the same. Isn't he? Use your head Merit.

MERIT:

(hesitates) I guess we're not doing him any favours carrying
him.

LEONARD:

The more we give him, the further he's going to sink.

MERIT:

He's had free place to live for the last fifteen years.

LEONARD:

And now I'd say it's time to let him go. We've got to cut him
loose.

MERIT:

(pause) What about mother?

LEONARD:

There's a place up there for seniors isn't there? She's
probably got some of her old batty friends in there. She's got
her pension. She'd probably welcome it. Those kids must be
driving her crazy. This is probably a very good time for this
to happen.

MERIT:
Maybe you're right.

LEONARD:
Settled. *(getting up)*

MERIT:
We'll talk to him after dinner. Together.

LEONARD:
I have some work to do. I was planning on heading out right after my culinary duties.

MERIT:
Oh Leonard.

LEONARD:
I can't talk to your brother. We live on different planets. You'll do fine. I'd better go check the ham.

SCENE TWO

Three hours later. The garden doors are open. Sunlight is pouring in. The sound of children's voices outside. Children's clothing, toys, sports equipment. FLORENCE and MERIT enter from outside. MERIT starts putting teacups on a tray. Always straightening.

FLORENCE:
That's one advantage of having so many kids. No problem getting a baseball game going.

MERIT:
You must get tired of all the noise.

FLORENCE:
It keeps me young. We don't see much of Leonard. He cooks the ham, he clears the table, he disappears.

MERIT:
He's very busy right now at work.

FLORENCE:
I thought you said things were slow

MERIT:

They were but now it's picking up.

FLORENCE:

Have you seen Corker lately?

MERIT:

Not since before we went to Costa Rica.

FLORENCE:

(quiet excitement) I had an idea, Merit. I've been thinking about it ever since the last time I was here. I thought Corker could come Up Home to live with us.

MERIT:

What?

FLORENCE:

Up Home.

MERIT:

Why on earth would he do that?

FLORENCE:

There's that little room in the attic. He could have that. I could find him work around town. I'm still the mayor's wife. I still have some favours to call in.

MERIT:

No.

FLORENCE:

I want to help him. It would give me something to do. The kids don't need me anymore. I've been thinking about it. I could make his lunch every day, send him off to his job. Make sure he has socks on. I could do that. I bet he'd like the wicker chair, the trees out back—the donut shop.

MERIT:

No! That's not going to happen.

FLORENCE:

Why not?

MERIT:

Because you can't just do things like that. There's a system in place...there's lots of red tape. It's complicated. You have no idea what his needs are. He's got...problems mother. He's got eczema and epilepsy and God knows what else up here. *(points to head)* He's a basket case to put it bluntly. And you don't need that in your life. Besides, he's probably straightened away quite nicely now. We haven't heard a peep from him in a month. No more nocturnal visits. No more calls. No news is good news. You look tired mom. Why don't you go lie down for a while before heading back.

FLORENCE:

(disappointed) Maybe I will.

MERIT:

The daybed in the study is all made up. Just make yourself comfortable.

FLORENCE:

All right.

> *MERIT walks out with another tray. FLORENCE walks around the fountain, sits down on the ledge at the back, fingers in the water. She is not obvious. GAL enters, looks around expectantly. MERIT returns. MERIT is dreading this conversation.*

GAL:

Did you talk with him?

MERIT:

We discussed it.

GAL:

And?

MERIT:

(hesitates then launches in) We don't think it makes economic sense.

GAL:

Sense?

MERIT:

We think it's an unacceptable outlay.

GAL:

A what?

MERIT:

You heard me.

GAL:

That lousy cheapskate just doesn't want to pay.

MERIT:

Now just a minute.

GAL:

And he doesn't have the courage to stick around another ten minutes to tell me.

MERIT:

It was a joint decision.

GAL:

Then you're both cheap cheapskates.

FLORENCE looks trapped. She covers her ears.

MERIT:

It's a bad investment.

GAL:

Everything has a pricetag. Even Up Home has a pricetag. I just figured it out. You're heartless. You're as cold as a dead cod on the beach in March. Here we've been thinking all these years that it's Leonard who's turned you around but it's been you all along! You're heartless to the core! Heartless!

MERIT:

Oh stop it!

GAL:

You don't give a damn about anyone but yourself and your goddamned bottom line! You were just too damn busy to even look in on your poor screwed up sister once in a while!

She had to come all the way Up Home to get a decent meal. Just too damn busy.

MERIT:

Don't say that.

GAL:

Just like you didn't have a minute to get up to see your old dad lying there staring at the ceiling—in five years, how many times did you make it? Twice!

MERIT:

I sent cards. I sent plants.

GAL:

Big deal! You abandoned him! And Serena! And now you want to ditch your old mom too 'cause she's a bad investment!

MERIT is devastated by this. FLORENCE starts singing loudly, a sixties Juliette song, hands over her ears. GAL and MERIT realize that she has been listening.

MERIT:

Ohmigod.

GAL:

Mom.

FLORENCE continues with the next loud verse.

MERIT:

Mother, I'm sorry. It sounded worse than….

GAL:

No it didn't.

FLORENCE:

I want to go home. Take me home Gal! Take me home.

MERIT:

Let me explain.

FLORENCE:

Take me home while I still have a home to go to.

GAL:

Glad to!

There is a thunderous pounding at the front door.

GAL:

Who the hell is that?

CORKER opens the doors and staggers in. His face is battered and bruised. He bumps into a table, knocks over everything.

FLORENCE:

(as if Jesus Christ himself has arrived) He's here!

GAL:

He's drunk.

MERIT:

No he's not. Grab him.

GAL tries holding him up.

GAL:

He's dead weight.

CORKER starts falling. MERIT grabs him and breaks his fall to the floor.

GAL:

Another liability has dropped in.

SCENE THREE

GLENNY is kneeling down inspecting CORKER. MERIT looks on anxiously.

GLENNY:

Too many drugs. Not enough food. I'd say he was double medicated. Maybe triple. The staff move through there like shit through a goose. Records go missing, get coffee spilled on them.... Got a bit of a tan down there, did you?

LEONARD enters.

LEONARD:
What's going on here?

GLENNY:
Someone must have left the door unlocked. He's been pretty closely watched since his rampage.

MERIT:
What rampage?

GLENNY:
Last week he snapped off thirty aerials in a parking lot.

MERIT:
(shocked) What?

GLENNY:
That was on top of trashing the Pit.

LEONARD:
It's not our concern.

MERIT:
He's lying on our livingroom floor Leonard! *(to GLENNY)* What brought this on?

GLENNY:
Don't ask me. I'm just a low life thug with a chintzy certificate....

MERIT:
(cuts him off) What brought this on?

GLENNY:
It could have been when you grabbed him by the collar and snarled at him like a rabid dog. That might have had a negative impact on his self image.

LEONARD:
That's enough.

GLENNY:
While your plane was taking off for Costa Rica, he was ripping up all the linoleum at the Pit. Then he trashed his

room, then he went into the bathroom and pulled the toilet from the wall.

LEONARD:
You heard me. That's enough!

CORKER suddenly jerks straight up, looks straight ahead, sheer terror in his eyes. He strikes out at LEONARD and hits him in the face. GLENNY restrains him.

CORKER:
No man! No man! No breakin' the glass, no rippin' the rug, no screaming, no peein' on the rug. No colourin' the wall, no no no throwing, no hittin'…. Tard! Tard! No goin' on da plane…goin'…Reena. Reena.

MERIT watches, wide-eyed in horror as his head drops again.

MERIT:
I'll see him again.

LEONARD:
The guy's gone off his nut.

MERIT:
(to GLENNY) Is he's still in line for Harbour House?

GLENNY:
Yup.

MERIT:
I'll see him once a week until he gets into Harbour House.

SCENE FOUR

The Park. CORKER enters, looks around expectantly, studies the ducks, gets out a bag of crumbs, starts feeding the ducks, talking to them quietly.

CORKER:
Quack. Quack. Quack.

MERIT enters in suit, high heels, sunglasses, stops, watches him.

CORKER:
Oink. Mooo.Quack quack quack!

She laughs. He does it some more. He watches her, happy.

CORKER:
Reena.

MERIT:
Did you come here with Serena?.

CORKER:
Quack quack quack quack! Quack?

MERIT:
Quack! *(MERIT laughs.)*

MERIT:
Quack quack quack quack!

CORKER/MERIT:
Quack Quack Quack!

He grabs her hand and pulls her towards a bench, takes her hand as if it is a great gift and leads her to the bench. They sit. She tries to pull her hand away. He holds on.

CORKER:
Tha...than...than...

MERIT:
What?

CORKER:
Thanyu....

MERIT:
Thank you?

CORKER:
For com...coming.

MERIT:
You're welcome. It's nice here.

CORKER:
Watch. Watch this.

CORKER closes his eyes, settles into holding her hand, sitting in the sun on the bench.

CORKER:
Lax. Re lax. Reena. Tan.

MERIT:
Tan?

CORKER:
Tan.

MERIT:
That's what the two of you did? You sat here holding hands getting a tan?

CORKER nods, settles in even more. Happy. MERIT looks self-conscious. She pulls away her hand.

MERIT:
I don't have much time. Let's feed the ducks. *(MERIT grabs the bag of breadcrumbs and jumps up)* It's the middle of the day. It's lunchtime. I don't want to sit. This isn't the beach. Come help me. Here you go duckies! Come and get it.

CORKER starts making burping sounds.

MERIT:
Stop that! Why do you do that? Why do you try to drive people away? Stop that or I'll leave.

CORKER stops. MERIT goes back to feeding the ducks

MERIT:
Look at those fat ones fighting over the scraps. Reminds me of the people I work with. Help me feed them.

CORKER shakes his head, sullen.

MERIT:
Suit yourself.

MERIT turns back to feeding the ducks.

MERIT:
I've been looking forward to this all week. A bit of fresh air.

CORKER notices her purse on the bench, opens it. He opens her wallet, takes some money, puts it in his pocket. CORKER takes out her compact, looks at himself, powders his nose. He finds a lipstick and starts putting it on like warpaint.

MERIT:

I've got the big job now. I've got a corner office with windows overlooking the harbour but none of them open. There's a parade of civil servants through my door asking me to run interference with the Premier, hoping their departments won't disappear before lunch. Meanwhile the Premier calls me five times a day to ask can we get out of this? Can we get cut that? Can we privatize the highways? What about the trees, the air around the Legislature? It never ends. He should meet my brother Gal. That might dampen his enthusiasm for free enterprise.

MERIT's cell phone rings on the park bench. CORKER jumps away from it, frightened. MERIT turns, sees what he is doing. Sees her wallet open. She puts everything back in her purse, grabs his arm, pulls him out of the park.

MERIT:

You're an animal!

SCENE FIVE

GLENNY's hole in the wall. MERIT drags CORKER in. CORKER dives deep into a pile of costumes, making muttering sounds.

MERIT:

I've had it. He shouldn't be out in public. He's a menace!

GLENNY:

You all right Cork?

CORKER nods.

GLENNY:

Just go. It was a hairbrained idea. Just go. He needs more that you can give him. You probably made things worse. He had his hopes up. It was a bad idea.

MERIT:

His hopes?

CORKER:

Cantchain cantchain…cantchain…no cantchain….

GLENNY:

He's fading. I've seen it before. He's like a canary in a mine.

MERIT:

What do you mean?

GLENNY:

He's going beyond where people can reach him. It's just too much for him. The only staffperson at the Pit who was half decent to him is gone. Serena's gone. He's alone.

MERIT:

No wonder. The way he acts.

GLENNY:

He just reflects back what comes into him. No one talks to him except the bully who just says suck me and fuck me and beat it retard. He's not gonna make it to Harbour House. He's gonna end up some night in a ditch.

She looks over at the pile of costumes.

CORKER:

Cannntchain cantchain….

MERIT:

I'll make some calls. Get some short term resources….

GLENNY:

There are no resources. Haven't you noticed? You don't listen do you? You don't see. You can only cut the pie so many ways and then it falls apart. I know what you're gonna say—we overspent in the seventies and we have to tighten our belts for the sake of our children. You don't have any children do you?

MERIT:

What does that matter?

GLENNY:

He loved going to the park with Serena. It was a magical
place with her. Serena filled him with pride and hope. She
was there for him!

MERIT:

What about me? I was there wasn't I?

GLENNY:

Did you hold his hand? Did you let him talk.

MERIT:

I don't need a performance evaluation every time I do a
good deed!

GLENNY:

Well how good was it? I bet you were checking your watch
every minute, fielding calls. That's not how Serena was. She
was really there for him!

MERIT:

Excuse me but killing oneself is hardly 'being there.'

GLENNY:

You're still mad about that aren't you?

MERIT:

Well it's rather academic at this....

GLENNY:

You think you're better than her don't you? What do you
think she did with her time?

MERIT:

I have no idea.

GLENNY:

She worked at the food bank. She bagged food. She made
soup for Hope Cottage. She visited shut-ins. She talked to
people all day long and she never closed a file on one of
them. She taught him how to play the piano. She gave him a
voice that he never had before. That's worth something isn't
it?

*

CORKER:
   Cantchain cantchain!

GLENNY:
   And she was going to AA.

MERIT:
   She was?

GLENNY:
   Five times a week.

CORKER:
   Cantchain cantchain!

MERIT:
   (new understanding) "God gives me the serenity to accept the things that I can't change...."

GLENNY:
   I used to me her meet there.

MERIT:
   You?

GLENNY:
   We walked home together some nights. She had a lot of things wrong with her towards the end.

MERIT:
   She did?

GLENNY:
   She was forgetting things. Street names. She was getting lost. It scared the hell out of her. That's why she stopped drinking. She was afraid that her mind was going. I don't know whether it was. I know she had regrets. I know that. I don't know what they were but I know they weighed on her. I think she was trying to make up for something in the past by helping Corker. He was like a connection. She was holding onto him for dear life—until she couldn't hang on any longer.

MERIT goes over to where CORKER is buried in the costumes and yanks him out.

MERIT:
No more stealing! Understand!

SCENE SIX

MERIT and LEONARD's house. The morning scramble to get out the door. MERIT digs through the pile of shoes at her desk. LEONARD is putting on cufflinks. Spring in his step. The glass doors are open.

LEONARD:
I need some new shirts. Since I've been going to the gym, my shirts are feeling a bit tight. Seen my briefcase?

MERIT:
Behind the couch.

LEONARD:
Where is my new striped tie?

MERIT:
Back of the closet door.

LEONARD:
Have you looked at the documents for the meeting?

MERIT:
I'll do that this morning.

LEONARD:
I was hoping maybe to have a little pre-meeting before the actual....

She looks at him.

LEONARD:
Well I mean we could just have lunch and if the conversation strayed in that direction....

MERIT:
That's hardly appropriate.

LEONARD:

Oh come on Merit. *(he notices stain on tie)* I can't wear this. Pesto sauce.

LEONARD leaves. A small cloth sack comes flying through the door and clatters to the floor. The contents of the sack scatter. It's all the stuff which CORKER has stolen.

MERIT:

(smiles) No stealin'.

She starts picking up the items. The jade elephant, the pewter horse. LEONARD comes back.

LEONARD:

What was that noise?

MERIT:

Corker returned the things he took from the house.

LEONARD:

Well that's big of him. Proof positive that he's not only violent and crazy but a thief.

MERIT:

(starts putting things back in their places) He returned them, Leonard.

LEONARD:

Well let's just have lunch together anyway. We won't talk business.

MERIT:

I can't. I told Corker I'd meet him in the park.

LEONARD:

You did that yesterday.

MERIT:

I know but I need to do it again today.

LEONARD:

Why?

MERIT:

Because he needs me right now.

LEONARD:
And I don't?

SCENE SEVEN

MERIT is standing in the park, waiting for CORKER. He jumps out at her, then crouches on the bench, scratching his wrist.

MERIT:
What's wrong with your hand? Show me.

CORKER:
Goway.

MERIT:
Is it eczema?

CORKER jumps up and walks away from her. He sits down on the ground, scratching at his hand.

CORKER:
Goway. GOWAY!

MERIT:
(quietly) Let me see it.

She holds out her hand to him.

MERIT:
Hand?

CORKER slowly holds his hand out towards her.

MERIT:
It's all raw! It's infected.

MERIT's phone rings. He pulls his hand away. He huddles down further.

CORKER:
Aughhhh!

She looks at the phone, she turns it off.

MERIT:

Gone. Phone gone.

He doesn't move. She takes the phone and throws it in the garbage can.

MERIT:

Phone gone.

CORKER slowly holds his hand out to her again. She takes it.

SCENE EIGHT

LEONARD is pacing, looking at his watch. MERIT comes in, blood on her scarf, looking the worse for wear.

LEONARD:

Where have you been? It's after nine o'clock. Are you alright? Merit? We waited for you 'til two o'clock. The Premier dazzled us with tales from the golf course. I kept sliding out to call you. No answer. No answer. By two, everyone looked pissed off. We called it quits. It was fucking embarrassing. Not to mention the fact that the Clerk happens to be my wife and I didn't have a clue where she was.

MERIT:

By two, I wasn't at the park.

LEONARD:

What's on your scarf?

MERIT:

Blood.

LEONARD:

You've been in an accident!

MERIT:

No. By two, I had taken Corker to Emergency. His hand was raw and infected. It had to be seen right away.

LEONARD:

We waited over an hour for you.

MERIT:

We waited two hours at the hospital before we even saw the intake worker. So much for right away.

LEONARD:

You sat in Emergency for two hours?

MERIT:

We were number eighty-five and they were only at sixty when we got there. What else could we do? A woman brought in a man with a head wound. She was holding a disposable diaper up to it to stop the bleeding. I thought surely he'd get seen right away but....no, they had to take a num....

LEONARD:

Why do you have blood on your scarf?

MERIT:

She asked if I would mind holding the diaper up to his head while she went to the bathroom....

LEONARD:

My God.

MERIT:

What could I say?

LEONARD:

No! You could have said No. What if he has AIDS?

MERIT:

That crossed my mind.

LEONARD:

It crossed your mind. Why didn't you dump Corker at Glenny's.

MERIT:

I didn't want to dump him.

LEONARD:

Why didn't you call? We wanted to start nailing some things down today. Things are moving incredibly fast.

MERIT:

Not in Emergency they're not.

LEONARD:

This is important Merit and you're making jokes. The Premier wants to green light this but the Clerk of the Cabinet is feeding ducks and sitting in Emergency with retards.

MERIT:

I didn't mind.

LEONARD:

What?

MERIT:

I didn't mind being there. I wanted to be there. The numbers kept clicking by getting closer and closer to eighty-five and we just sat there holding hands. I felt legitimate, useful. The migraine I've been fighting for the last decade went away. Between the blood-soaked diaper and Corker's raw hand. Gone.

LEONARD:

Are you alright?

MERIT:

Around seventy-five I starting thinking about Serena. She worked at the food bank, Leonard. She made soup for Hope Cottage. Every day when we were sitting in traffic jams in front of the place, she was in there making lunch. And she was going to AA. We never knew that, Leonard.

LEONARD:

So?

MERIT:

When the police called and told you they'd found her and you went over there Leonard, where was she?

LEONARD:
   What does it matter?

MERIT:
   I want to know.

LEONARD:
   Well, she was lying on the floor and her hair was…her face was kind of…she didn't look great Merit. She was…dead.

MERIT:
   What was she thinking about when she took all those pills?

LEONARD:
   I don't know.

MERIT:
   Why did she do it, Leonard?

   LEONARD moved toward her. She pulls away.

LEONARD:
   Now where are you going?

MERIT:
   Out!

LEONARD:
   It's after nine o'clock!

MERIT:
   I'm going for a walk.

SCENE NINE

   GLENNY's hole in the wall. GLENNY is working late, moving about slowly, very carefully, muttering to himself. He is looking for something.

GLENNY:
   Where are ya? You were right here a minute ago.

   MERIT enters. GLENNY looks up.

GLENNY:

What are you doing here?

GLENNY lurches to one side, then rights himself.

MERIT:

You're drunk!

GLENNY:

Nope. Just tired and emotional. *(GLENNY finally locates the lost mickey under a report. He holds it up, grimaces. He polishes the last drop from the bottle.)* No more referrals…restructural analysis. Other alternatives. *(drops letter, picks up empty bottle)* Shoulda bought two of 'em.

He stumbles, MERIT has to help him.

MERIT:

What are you talking about?

GLENNY:

Harbour House is closing. You musta heard. Came outa yer budget. Everything's closing, freezing, re…re…structuring…changing…whole new regime, end of the year. Whole new world. Shrink shrink shrink. All just shrinking right up to nothing. Word has it American company's gonna take over bloody everything…gonna run it "state of the art"—whatever the hell that means…. Ask your husband. Maybe he knows. He's representing the bastards.

GLENNY crashes to the floor, knocks over all the Lego. MERIT cleans it up.

GLENNY:

You think the workers got low morale now, wait 'til they have their wages cut in half? It's all just slipping away….

MERIT:

They're leaders in medical management.

GLENNY:

They run jails in the United States! What does that have to to do with the mentally handicapped! Who is this serving? The public good? If Serena were here, she'd hoist a banner, grab a bullhorn, lead a protest. Always raging. Always fighting. She'd take to the streets, she'd be out front singing: "We shall overcome, we shall overcome, we shall overcome some day." She was a glory to the world. That big bright smile on her face, filling people with hope, laughing, always laughing though she wasn't laughing much towards the end. She was lonely. I could tell. She was scared towards the end. I could see it in her face. Fear had crept into that beautiful face. I was going to ask her out that very night—I'd screwed up my courage and I was going to see if she'd go to the races—but I was too late. Never put things off. *(he looks at the bottle)* And now who's gonna lead the parade? I can't do it. I wish I could. But I'm just yer lowly footsoldier. And no one even thinks that's important anymore. Guess it doesn't really matter. Harbour House wasn't that shit hot anyway. Just a couple of cuts away from being another Pit. It was at the mercy of the assholes with the red pencils too.

MERIT:
What about Corker?

GLENNY:
Dunno. Why don't you go find out. What was it she always said? Light up some corners with your curiosity. Seek wisdom and tell the truth.

SCENE TEN

MERIT and LEONARD's house. LEONARD enters.

LEONARD:
Thanks a lot.

MERIT:
I had some questions. The Premier hired me to give him good advice.

LEONARD:
Here I am trying to stick handle the deal of the decade and my wife is across the table sabotaging me.

MERIT:

Your wife? I'm a bit more than that aren't I? I'm the Clerk of the Cabinet.

LEONARD:

Not today you weren't. You were like one of those crazy dames from those women's organizations you see on the evening news—with that deeply concerned look on your face—and believe me it wasn't flattering. These people are world leaders in human services delivery.

MERIT:

Prisons.

LEONARD:

Well they're full of humans.

MERIT:

There are problems in their prisons.

LEONARD:

And they're working through them.

MERIT:

Higher fences, tighter security.

LEONARD:

What's wrong with that?

MERIT:

They've never run homes for mentally handicapped adults. That's what we're contracting them to do.

LEONARD:

They're moving into that field. They're going through a period of adjustment. They tried to answer the questions.

MERIT:

No they didn't. They talked all around them. They didn't use the word 'home,' Leonard. They never did. Did you notice that? It was 'facility,' or 'premise,' or 'installation.' Who wants to live in an installation?

LEONARD:

This could save almost a billion dollars in ten years. It will save money.

MERIT:

And it will make money too won't it?

LEONARD:

You wanted to streamline things Merit. You wanted to make things more efficient.

MERIT:

I looked at the figures Leonard. They're making a fortune on their prisons. Warehousing humans is a very lucrative business. What does that have to do with the public interest?

LEONARD:

That's the way it's always been. Don't say you haven't noticed. It hasn't bothered you up 'til now.

MERIT:

I didn't have a Corker in my life 'til now. There won't be a Harbour House. He'll be an inmate. He won't have any choice.

LEONARD:

Who the hell's got choices? Do you think I want to be wheeling and dealing for companies like this? But that's the name of the game. He hired you to be ruthless.

MERIT:

And why did he hire you?

LEONARD:

What?

MERIT:

They thought they could get a leg up by hiring the husband of the Clerk.

LEONARD:

Well what if they did? How do you think you got started? Do you think it was your stunning personality? How do you think that happened? Because my uncle put a word in, backed up with a big donation at election time. That's how you got started. That's how everything gets started. Don't act like you were born yesterday. Don't start acting like a MacPhee, self-destructing every step of the way. Pull yourself together.

MERIT:

Remember the high hopes we had when we started out? I was going to work for the public good and make my father proud. You used to sit for hours reading Proust. You were the dreamer. You were always late for everything. I bought you your first watch. You didn't even want to be a lawyer. You just wanted to be a judge. You were going to be a family court judge because you loved kids.

LEONARD:

Yeah, well we didn't have any of those did we? We were too damn busy.

MERIT:

You're right Leonard. We were too damn busy. I just want to stop. I don't understand anymore. It's all just starting to float around on me.

LEONARD:

Listen to me Merit. You've worked incredibly hard. You got your budget in. You've done well. You're the talk of the town. You deserve a break. Just stop for a while. Get your ducks in a row. *(he takes her hands)* Will you do that?

SCENE ELEVEN

MERIT brings in a tray with tea, cups. In the centre there is a brass goblet. She looks controlled but fragile. She puts an envelope into the brass goblet on the tray. Arranges it in just the right way. The doorbell rings.

MERIT:

Let them in.

LEONARD goes to the door, lets in GAL and FLORENCE. GAL looks at LEONARD coldly.

LEONARD:
May I take your coats?

GAL:
I'll leave mine on.

FLORENCE lets LEONARD help her with her coat, looks cautiously at her daughter.

GAL:
What's the occasion? It's not Easter or Thanksgiving. No one's died. Ever heard of phones?

LEONARD:
We didn't want to phone. We wanted to tell you in person.

GAL:
(looks from LEONARD to his sister) You've got another big promotion. You're the queen now.

MERIT:
(ignoring him) Sit right here. Right in front of the table. The place of honour. *(leads FLORENCE to a chair)* I've taken some time off to do some reassessing, prioritizing. Leonard and I have revisited the whole topic of Up Home.

GAL:
Too late for that. The movers are coming Monday. The wreckers the next day. We'll be in the trailer park that night. It's too friggin late for....

MERIT:
We still think that we made the right decision to let the house go. But we feel there is more we can do to make mom comfortable and happy....

LEONARD:
And so, without further ado....

MERIT hands FLORENCE the brass goblet.

LEONARD:

Open it.

FLORENCE takes the envelope out of the goblet, opens it and finds a key.

MERIT:

There's a card too. Read it.

GAL:

What does it say?

FLORENCE:

"Welcome to Hawthorne Heights. Elegant suites, well-appointed, beautifully furnished…."

MERIT:

Go on.

FLORENCE closes up the brochure, sits with her hands crossed, stares at fountain.

MERIT:

Go on. *(MERIT takes the brochure)* "…spectacular gardens in the centre of the city. The prestige address for gracious senior living." And you have a suite there starting next Monday. 36B. It will all work like clockwork. You'll all move out of the house at the same time. It'll be one hell of a day but then it'll all be done. 36B.

Neither GAL nor FLORENCE show any reaction.

MERIT:

You're thinking about the cost, aren't you? Leonard and I are looking after that. Don't even think about it. There's a doorman. There's a state of the art security system. Five-piece baths with brass fixtures. It is beautifully furnished with turn of the century antiques. There's a waiting list into the millennium and I got you in next week.

GAL:

And you say it's furnished?

MERIT:

Beautifully furnished! There's a love seat, a rose velvet love seat to die for....

GAL:

She's got furniture. They were going to let her bring her own furniture to the place Up Home.

MERIT:

Well she can bring a couple of pieces if she likes. They don't mind that.

GAL:

A couple.

MERIT:

One or two.

GAL:

For all those big bucks you think you could at least have your own....

MERIT:

Oh for God's sake! There isn't one piece of furniture left that doesn't have jam marks all over it from your....

LEONARD:

(jumps in) The less furniture, the easier the move. You could probably bring everything down in the van, maybe just with a roof rack.

GAL:

We don't have a roof rack

LEONARD:

I think there's one somewhere out in the garage. *(to GAL)* Shall we go look?

GAL hesitates. LEONARD nudges GAL.

LEONARD:

Shall we?

LEONARD and GAL leave. MERIT paces around watching her mother. FLORENCE goes and sits by the fountain, her hand in the water.

MERIT:

I know it's sudden but I thought you'd be over the moon about this. If you knew how many people would kill to get into Hawthorne Heights....

FLORENCE:

Where is he?

MERIT:

I don't know. I...I had to step back. My health was suffering. My work. I was getting physically ill. We did everything we could. I have no contact with him anymore. Take a look at these pictures. How lovely it is. You're going to have some important neighbours. Senator MacKay's mother. There's a former Supreme Court judge. You're going to live like a queen there. You've earned it.

FLORENCE:

How?

MERIT:

Well...you've worked hard all your life.

FLORENCE:

Aren't we all tightening our belts?

MERIT:

Well, yes, but...I've worked hard. I should be able to put my mother anywhere I want.

FLORENCE:

Put me?

MERIT:

I didn't mean 'put.' That was a bad choice of words. This is a gift that I want to give to you. I want you to enjoy the remaining years of your life in a nice....

FLORENCE:

What about what I want? Nobody asked me what I wanted.

MERIT:
Well I guess I didn't think I could go very wrong with the best.

FLORENCE :
What happened to the last poor soul in 36B? Did they kick her out to let me in? Or did she croak?

MERIT:
I don't know exactly how that works.

FLORENCE:
But you pushed your weight around. You said that. You seem proud of that.

MERIT:
I am not proud of it. I just have quite a bit of influence and I wanted to make you happy. And Gal does too. This will be a big load off his mind too when he starts to think of anyone else but himself.

FLORENCE is looking down at the water.

FLORENCE :
I read a funny little article about grannie suites. Knock out a wall or two and build on and Bob's your uncle.

MERIT:
Mother....

FLORENCE:
Well it didn't even look like it was that difficult to do.

MERIT:
Who ever heard of attaching a grannie suite to a mobile home!

FLORENCE:
If Serena were here, I could go live with her. I could help her out.

MERIT:
Well she's not.

FLORENCE:
No Pit.

MERIT:
  What did you say?

FLORENCE:
  (finally) I don't want to be a bother to anyone.

MERIT:
  Then just do this for me mom. It'll be for the best for everyone. Here, take a look at the pictures.

SCENE TWELVE

  It's night. The sidewalk. CORKER enters, carrying FLORENCE's suitcases. FLORENCE enters, in travelling clothes, reading a map.

FLORENCE:
  (studying a map) Montreal. That's where we'll start. Montreal. They speak French there. I know a bit. Parlez-vous français, mon petit chou.

CORKER:
  (tries this out) Chew.

FLORENCE:
  Say 'bonjour.'

CORKER:
  Say Bonger. Bonger! Bonger!

FLORENCE:
  Good. Say 'merci.'

CORKER:
  Merci.

FLORENCE:
  Very good.

CORKER:
  (pleased with himself) Merci! MERCI!

FLORENCE:
  We'll start in Montreal. Spend the weekend there, eat french onion soup, croissants. We can drink some wine, eh? Ooh la la!

CORKER:
Yessss! Ooh la la!

FLORENCE:
Then get back on the plane, just keep going, right across the country to Vancouver, the other ocean. We'll buy our tickets, check our luggage, get on the plane, strap on our seat belts and put our seat backs up, eat cookies, drink coke. Go to the little washrooms. Go up front and visit the pilot....

CORKER:
(pretends he has on headphones) Fasten seatbelts! Fasten seatbelts!

FLORENCE:
This will be a grand adventure Corker. We're going on a plane.

CORKER:
Goin' on da plane! Goin' on da plane!

FLORENCE:
They won't have to tell me to go lie down any more 'cause I'll be gone. I'll just get right out of their hair. Save everyone a pisspot full of money. No more basket cases.

CORKER:
No baskets!

FLORENCE:
No baskets Cork. Or people who look a little different or think a little different. It's two for the road for us Corker.

CORKER's face is full of delight, then it turns to fear, alarm.

SCENE THIRTEEN

MERIT and GAL are in the livingroom. GAL has a note in his hand.

GAL:
(reads) "Au revoir. We'll send for my pension cheques. See you sometime next year." Omigod.

LEONARD roars in, agitated.

LEONARD:

What is it? You alright Merit. What is it?

MERIT:

Leonard....

LEONARD:

This better be good. I was in the middle of a senior partners' meeting with Slamemshut. I just happen...I just happen to have the deal of the century right here in the palm of my hand....

GAL:

Who cares about your goddamned deal of the century?

GAL hands him the note.

LEONARD:

(reads) "Au revoir. We'll send for my pension cheques. See you sometime next year." Jesus.

MERIT:

Mother's taken Corker and they've gone off somewhere.

LEONARD:

Somewhere?

GAL:

They've been gone for twenty-four hours. She could be lying in a snowdrift. She could be at the bottom of the harbour.

MERIT:

What are we going to do Leonard?

LEONARD:

I don't know. Let's just calm down.

GAL:

(crosses himself) Jesus Mary and Joseph...my seventy-five-year-old mother is wandering around out there and you tell me to calm down.

LEONARD:

They won't get far. They're an odd couple. The police will spot them. How the hell did you let her just walk out like that?

GAL:

We were trying to get the twin beds into the truck. We had to repack everything. She must have gone out the back gate. She must've taken the five o'clock bus to the city.

MERIT:

And you didn't notice she was gone?

GAL:

No! I didn't! I was too busy stuffing every single solitary thing we own into a truck two sizes too small.

LEONARD:

How did she know where to find Corker?

GAL:

We drove him home one night.

LEONARD:

Why did they let him just go off with her like that?

GAL:

Why not? She's a nice old lady! She's my mother!

MERIT:

She's my mother too!

The phone rings. LEONARD jumps for it.

LEONARD:

Hello? *(listens)* Circus? Why the hell would I want to go to a circus?

LEONARD slams down the phone.

GAL:

I should have noticed something was going on with her. I should have noticed. It's my fault the house is gone. In the wink of an eye. Gone. Two hours to level it. Nothing left. I've screwed up everything. You name it, I screwed it up. And now my old mom is wandering around out there with her suitcases. I've gotta take a piss.

GAL leaves.

MERIT:

I didn't hear her Leonard. She said: "I read a funny little article about grannie suites. Just knock out a couple of walls and Bob's your uncle." I didn't even hear her.

LEONARD:

It'll all work out. It'll just turn out to be another wacky chapter in the life of the family MacPhee.

MERIT:

Don't say things like that anymore.

LEONARD:

What?

MERIT:

Don't put my family down anymore.

LEONARD:

I was just joking. You do it all the time.

MERIT:

It's not funny. My dignified old mother is out in the middle of nowhere....

The phone rings. MERIT jumps for it. GAL comes running back in.

MERIT:

Hello. *(listens)* Yes. Yes. Yes. They're in Montreal? He what? Is he alright? Ohmigod. Thank you. Yes. Thank you.

MERIT hangs up the phone.

MERIT:

They're at the airport in Montreal.

LEONARD:

(relieved) Thank God.

MERIT:

Corker didn't have his medication. He had a seizure. When they found them, she was trying to stop his head from banging against the floor. They're holding Corker 'til social services comes and gets him....

GAL:

And mom?

MERIT:

She bought a ticket to Las Vegas—leaving at nine tonight.

She looks at GAL.

GAL:

(shakes head) Don't look at me. I've done enough damage. I've got a wife and kids sitting in a mobile home with no power. I'm outa here.

LEONARD goes for his coat.

LEONARD:

There's a six forty to Montreal. I'll go and get her.

MERIT:

Leonard? It's my turn.

MERIT starts to leave.

LEONARD:

Call me from the airport.

SCENE FOURTEEN

A waiting room, Montreal airport. FLORENCE is sitting by herself, surrounded by her suitcases and bags full of tacky airport souvenirs. MERIT enters and finds her mother.

MERIT:

(relieved) There you are. We were so worried about you. You gave us a terrible scare.

FLORENCE:

Go away.

MERIT:

Mother, I just took a plane here to get you. I'm not going away.

FLORENCE:

You wasted your time. And your money. Go away.

FLORENCE holds tightly to all her bags.

MERIT:

Can I at least see what you've bought?

FLORENCE lets go of one of the strings of her shopping bags. MERIT looks in. She pulls out some souvenirs—A glass bubble from Niagara Falls, a Montreal Expos pennant.

MERIT:

For the kids? I guess you'd better come home and give them to them.

FLORENCE:

Don't talk to me like a child. Go away. Just leave me alone. What does it matter where I am? I couldn't even stop his head from smashing against the floor.

MERIT:

I'm sure it's not the first time.

FLORENCE:

I was going to take him on an adventure and it turned into a nightmare. I just made things worse. Don't waste your time on me.

FLORENCE grabs back her souvenirs, stuffs them in the bag.

MERIT:

Mother, you can't stay here.

FLORENCE:

I'm not going to stay here. I'm going to Las Vegas to gamble myself silly.

MERIT:

No you're not. You're coming home.

FLORENCE:

No one has a home anymore. Gal's in a trailer, Corker's in an installation. You're in a museum. I'm in 36B.

MERIT:

You make it sound like a disease.

FLORENCE:

Isn't it?

MERIT:

No, it's an elegant, well-appointed home for...older people who....

FLORENCE:

Who nobody wants. Nobodies with money.

MERIT:

That's what you think I am, isn't it? A nobody with money.

FLORENCE:

I loved the names we gave you children. Serena, Merit, Galahad. They were like jewels. Full of possibilities.

MERIT:

They were hard names to live up to.

FLORENCE:

They were full of ideals, your names. Your father was full of ideals. Our family was full of ideals. We were a model for our community. Everyone looked up to the MacPhees. I still have calendars from those years when he was a mayor. Every day was filled with engagements. We were sought after. We were envied. We were a happy family. Weren't we? Your dad always said the sun found her. They were very close. Do you remember when we all went to the Mayor's Levy on New Year's Day and he would get Serena to dance for everyone.

MERIT:

That was a long time ago.

FLORENCE:

She had a way with plants. Everywhere she lived she had a little jungle. She made everything alive around her. She was serene.

MERIT:

She went up and down like a roller coaster. She was anything but serene.

FLORENCE:

She was emotional. She had big feelings about everything.

MERIT:

(increasing frustration) She was a drunk, mother. She was two steps away from being a bag lady.

FLORENCE :

She drank because she cared so much. She didn't care about material things.

MERIT:

She was emotionally unstable, mother.

FLORENCE:

She saw things that other people didn't.

MERIT:

She killed herself mother.

FLORENCE:

(pause) I know. *(smiles wistfully)* I loved the names I gave you children.

MERIT:

I tried my whole life to live up to my name—Merit—for God's sake—you and your damn high faluting names! And your standards. And your ideals! But I never did live up to it. Neither did she. The last time I saw her was the night dad died. She staggered into our house, pissed to the gills, to tell me that my lifestyle, my husband, my clothes, everything I did was full of shit. All because I wasn't there by his bedside like the rest of you. Like I wasn't somehow a dutiful daughter. How was I to know he was going to die that night? It had been five years! There were no signs, no turns for the worse. How was I to know? You know why I stopped going to see him? Because I couldn't bear to see him like that. Lying there. Staring off at the potted plant. I couldn't bear it. I couldn't do a thing. I couldn't fix it. And I couldn't fix her either. I hated the midnight calls, the wrath, the ups and downs. It was wrecking my marriage, my life. I had to let her go. And then she went and killed herself before I even had a chance to….

FLORENCE:
Say goodbye.

A moment between them—a realization of shared grief.

FLORENCE:
She came Up Home the weekend before she died. She came into the kitchen and sat in the rocker and looked out at the garden for the longest time and said, "If I had Merit's determination and her three-piece suits, I could change the world."

MERIT:
She said that?

FLORENCE:
She did. She lived in your shadow, just like I lived in your father's. And when I was finally going to be my own person, not just someone herding a flock of children, or the Mayor's dutiful wife, when I was finally going to get out of there, he had the stroke. You know how I felt for the next five years, caring for him? Pissed right off.

MERIT:
You did?

FLORENCE:
The night he died, I went into my bedroom and did a little dance. I was glad he was gone. There. I've said it.

FLORENCE gets up, grabs her shopping bags.

MERIT:
Where are you going?

FLORENCE:
I've got a plane to catch!

SCENE FIFTEEN

A month later. MERIT enters the house, hurriedly takes off her hat and coat. She takes off her high-heeled shoes, pitches them across the room. She walks over to the piano, starts moving it around.

MERIT:
Love life. Live every day. Find the joy, chase it down. Thank you sister for your old hippie clichés. And thanks for your final pronouncements about stray cats. That's what the world needs now—better fed cats. And stand on your head. Who the hell has time to stand on their head?

LEONARD enters, going through the mail.

LEONARD:
Visa bill.

MERIT:
Screw Visa.

LEONARD:
Mastercard due.

MERIT:
Screw Mastercard.

LEONARD:
(looks out the window) Gal just took out all the rose bushes with the truck.

MERIT:
I can't deal with that now. It's almost five o'clock. I'd better call in.

LEONARD hesitates.

LEONARD:
Why bother?

He exits to the kitchen. MERIT picks up the phone.

MERIT:
(to phone) P.V.? I've just got back from the press conference. The family's on the way. I guess you could say that the universe is starting to unfold as it should.

LEONARD:
(*returns with a a tray of Aspirins, Rolaids and water*) Unravel.

MERIT:
Could you get me some Aspirins and Rolaids.

   LEONARD puts the tray beside her. GAL enters carrying a bedpost.

MERIT:
(*to phone*) I handed out the reports on Slamemshut, the lawsuits against them in four states. The reporters had a field day, best story they've had since the toilet seat scandal. He hired me to give him advice and that's what I did.

GAL:
I guess you hear it here first. Action central.

LEONARD:
Not anymore.

   FLORENCE wanders in, wearing a sunhat which says: 'Las Vegas' and a bag of Las Vegas souvenirs.

GAL:
Where do you want this?

FLORENCE:
Right over there, by the fountain.

MERIT:
(*to phone*) Tell Gilbert if he wants the 'Globe and Mail,' he has to pay for it himself.

FLORENCE:
Who is she talking to?

LEONARD:
Her ex-executive assistant.

FLORENCE:
I thought that's what you were.

LEONARD:
No, Florence. I am her husband.

   FLORENCE is surprised by his tone.

GAL:

I don't know about this mom. With all that water running, it might make you...you know....

FLORENCE:

What?

GAL:

Wet the bed.

FLORENCE:

It'll be fine for tonight then it'll go into the spare room.

MERIT:

(to phone) Tell him the fig tree is mine and so is the Sheila Butler litho. And the air filter and the humidifier.

GAL:

I hear your law firm got the bum's rush from Slamemshut. Your deal of the century went west. That musta hurt. Guys like that—you make too much heat, they walk away. Believe me. I've been there. I live there. I've got a permanent address there. *(pause)* I've been thinking about getting into the Offshore. That's where it's all happening eh? Know if there's any money around for retraining?

LEONARD:

No idea. Merit, get off the phone.

MERIT:

(to phone) Tell him the delegates from China are arriving on Friday and there'll be an international incident if doesn't work out this time.

GAL:

Will she get a package?

LEONARD:

Let's hope so. Or we'll be out at the trailer park with you.

GAL:

(he is watching his sister) Gotta hand it to her. She stood up to the screwball. She spoke her mind. Gutsy, eh?

LEONARD stands watching her.

LEONARD:
  (grudgingly) Yeah.

  GLENNY enters with a green garbage bag filled with clothes, knocks into LEONARD. They both tense up.

GLENNY:
  So where do I put this stuff?

  CORKER enters, runs over to the piano, starts playing.

MERIT:
  (gestures) In there.

LEONARD:
  Hang up Merit!

GAL:
  Well I guess that's everything.

FLORENCE:
  Then you'd better go now. *(GAL hesitates).* You've got a long drive back. Go!

  GAL gives FLORENCE a kiss. MERIT waves at him. GAL walks to the door, leaves.

MERIT:
  (to phone) Tell Gilbert if he wants to make sure the Chinese delegation makes it to the World Trade and Convention Centre, he should pick them up himself. That'll be the only way it will happen. And hide his golfclubs for…. Oh what do I care? Tell him the ulcers come with the job!

  She hangs up the phone, looks around at the mess. CORKER and GLENNY bring inbarbells, FLORENCE brings in an afghan and places it on a chair. LEONARD comes by, takes it off, puts it on her bed. FLORENCE comes back in and puts it back on the chair. GLENNY and CORKER go out, come back with more green garbage bags full of CORKER's belongings. The place fills with junk. GLENNY and CORKER do their high five.

GLENNY:
  Gonna head out now. Take it easy Cork. There's an emergency at the bridge. *(to MERIT)* Call if you need me.

MERIT:

Don't worry. I will.

GLENNY and CORKER do a final high five and a somewhat awkward hug. GLENNY leaves. LEONARD picks up a barbell.

LEONARD:

Help me with this stuff will ya?

CORKER and FLORENCE pick up CORKER's stuff, head into the study. MERIT, left alone, goes to the piano, tentatively. She puts her hand on the top.

MERIT:

Roll your corncob in butter. Lick the plate clean. Love life. Live every day. Find the joy. Chase it down. Flat out...scared shitless.

LEONARD, FLORENCE and CORKER come back. They stare at the mess before them.

LEONARD:

Now what do we do?

MERIT:

Let's go dancing.

LEONARD:

What?

MERIT:

Dancing. Remember that?

CORKER:

Yes!

MERIT:

We used to do that, Leonard. Remember? *(turns to CORKER and FLORENCE)* You two get settled. We'll be back around midnight

LEONARD:

(surprised) Midnight!

MERIT:

Maybe one.

LEONARD:
  One!

  MERIT kisses LEONARD.

CORKER:
  No kissin'!

  MERIT goes over and kisses CORKER on the cheek.

MERIT:
  Good night Corker.

CORKER:
  (holding his cheek where she kissed him) Night.

MERIT:
  Night mom.

  CORKER and FLORENCE watch them leave.

FLORENCE:
  Change the world. *(turns to CORKER)* I'll make the pizza.

  CORKER sits down at the piano. Plays a couple of notes.

CORKER:
  Home.

  CORKER starts to play 'Ode to Joy' with both hands. Lights go down. Rock music from first scene in Act One comes up. Lights go up for bow.

THE END